Cultures in Conflict

The Union Desecration Of Southern Churches and Cemeteries

(Plus much more)

by Charles A. Jennings

Published by:
TRUTH IN HISTORY

An Outreach of
KINGDOM TREASURE MINISTRIES
P.O. Box 808
Owasso, Oklahoma 74055-0808

www.truthinhistory.org

Acknowledgements

I want to express my deepest appreciation in the preparation of this third edition to my wife Marylee, for her invaluable assistance. For her patience and ability in computer work, typing the text, correcting errors and other tasks in making this book possible.

Copyright 2001
Charles A. Jennings
All rights reserved

Second Printing April 2002

Third Printing August 2012

ISBN #978-0-9829817-2-6

Truth wears no mask, seeks neither place nor applause, bows to no human shrine; yields to neither fear nor favor; all she asks is a hearing!

This book is dedicated
in honor and reverence
to the men, women and
children of the
Confederate States of America -
who with genuine faith and courage
withstood all the ravages of war
while trying to preserve
Southern Culture,
Constitutional Government
and
Biblical Christianity.

"If I ever disown, repudiate, or apologize for the cause for which Lee fought and Jackson died, let the lightnings of heaven rend me, and the scorn of all good men and true women be my portion. Sun, moon, stars, all fall on me when I cease to love the Confederacy. 'Tis the Cause, not the fate of the Cause, that is glorious!'"

Major R.E. Wilson, CSA

"All that was, or is now desired is that error and injustice be excluded from the text books of the schools and from the literature brought into our homes; that the truth be told, without exaggeration and without omission; truth for its own sake and for the sake of history, and that the generations to come after us not be left to bear the burden of shame and dishonor unrighteously laid upon the name of their noble sires."

Rev. James P. Smith
Last survivor of the staff of Lt. Gen. Thomas J. "Stonewall" Jackson

God made the right stronger than might,
Millions would trample us down in their pride.
Lay thou their legions low, roll back the ruthless foe,
Let the proud spoiler know God's on our side.
Let the proud spoiler know God's on our side.

(Third Verse)

Foreword

This small volume will be an eye-opener to many who wonder about the causes of the great War Between the States. Charles A. Jennings goes down below the surface reasons that are usually given and uncovers the foundation cause. A civilization, a culture is always based upon a system of beliefs, a religion. This is true because cultures and civilizations are made up of individuals and individuals are governed by their concept (or misconcept) of God, who He is, and what He is.

An accurate and reasonable understanding of the divine Being by man can only come through revelation. Because puny man (regardless of his I.Q.) Can only understand the Almighty as the Almighty chooses to reveal Himself. Psalm 19 tells us that He does this in two ways: through His creation and through His written Word. The human philosopher or religious leader who relies only on natural revelation always falls far short of understanding who and what God is and His will.

The Protestant Reformation brought this great truth to the top - that our authority is God's breathed out Word, the Holy Bible, which, in turn, sets forth the Lord Jesus Christ as the ultimate, final revelation of God to man (Hebrews 1:3).

The Bible, therefore, becomes our authority in all matters of faith and of practice, of what to believe and how to live. It is the yardstick by which we may measure what is true and what is false, what is right and what is wrong, what is salvation and its results as well as an accurate description of damnation and its consequences. Nowhere was that position so strongly, so tenaciously held as in the South. The religious liberal might sneer at the term "Bible Belt," but the Southern Christian considers it the crowned jewel of all titles used to describe Dixie.

In general terms, this was not the situation in the North and particularly, the Northeast, which then, as now, dominates so much of Northern thinking. Any follower of the television news media soon realizes that any event that occurs in Boston or New York is of far greater importance than if it occurred anywhere else in the country.

New England had the good fortune of being settled by the Puritans of England. These God-fearing, noble people who endured such heart-rendering hardships to practice and propagate a Bible faith had much to be admired. They, however, had the great misfortune of having a posterity that apostatized, that is, fell away from that faith. Churches that were built to preach the Gospel of the Lord Jesus Christ in the seventeenth and eighteenth century by the nineteenth century were preaching another gospel which is not a Gospel at all. The social gospel of unconverted men replaced the gospel of the Bible and consequently, when the Bible did not support the new message, the Bible was forsaken and in many instances despised. This departure from God's Word always brings corruption and a perverted view of life. The United States Constitution framed by God-fearing men was denounced as a "compact with hell." The Scriptures fared no better in the hands of such people.

As the Christian faith grew weaker in the Northeast, it manifestly grew stronger in the South. This produced two different cultures which are antagonist and will always be incompatible. (See II Corinthians 6:14-18).

It is a fact of history that those who depart from the faith of their fathers hate those who hold to "the old-time religion." Have you noticed, reader, that the same crowd who ridicules the orthodox Christian faith are the same ones who support the "cultural cleansing" of the South? The same folk who hate the Southern Confederacy are usually the ones who hold Biblical Christianity in contempt. It is no wonder, for in many ways they are inseparable.

The author sets before us a record that saddens the heart of all good people regardless of their geographical location. The fiendish desire to destroy, to desecrate, to defile the houses of Christian worship can only display a hatred conceived in the bowels of hell. To exhume the moldering bodies of Southern departed loved ones for *sport* or for *spoil* is an act so low that only the disciples of Satan could approve. No wonder there was a War - a war that cannot be explained only by politics, finances or slavery. No! The issues were and are much deeper. It was a matter of how shall we live: by faith or by man's unstable ideas, by God's Holy Word or by humanistic philosophy, by trusting in Christ as Lord and Saviour or searching for some deliverer in a man-made program.

Read these accounts of history. Some will know of other churches being willfully destroyed or desecrated, of graves purposely opened. If you are one of these, please contact the author. Perhaps, a second edition could be much enlarged. Do not let these events die with our generation. Our people need to know what happened.

The question for us today is: whose side am I on? Do I stand on Christ the Solid Rock? Or, do I prefer "sinking sand?" You understand, I trust: the War is not over, but the victory is assured.

Rev. Charles Estell Baker, D.D.
6 *years* - Chaplain-in-Chief
Sons of Confederate Veterans
29 *years* - Pastor
Center Point Independent Church
38 *years* - A Sinner Saved by Grace
Birmingham, Alabama
2 April A.D. 2001

<u>INTRODUCTION</u>

My interest in the subject of the Union desecration of Southern property and the verbal, physical, mental and moral abuses heaped upon the Southern people goes back over forty years.

While doing library research for a high school assignment, I discovered the inhumane treatment committed against the innocent civilians of the South during the War for Southern Independence of 1861-1864. This new found information was emotionally disturbing at the time and remains so to this day. In this 'human rights' atmosphere in which we now live, without doubt the perpetrators of those crimes would be tried and prosecuted before a War Crimes Tribunal. Because of the prevailing winds of anti-Southern prejudice that are now blowing through academic, political and even religious circles, the facts of these brutal atrocities are hidden in dusty history books and when revealed are relegated to a place of unimportance.

Over the years, my interest increased in these matters, especially after learning of both my paternal and maternal Southern ancestry and the part they played in trying to preserve our traditional way of life which existed in ante-bellum Southern society.

It has not been an easy task to find material that recounts the desecration of Southern churches and cemeteries. Many first-hand accounts were not written down or not properly preserved in order to document the vile acts committed by Union military forces in their ravage and plunder of the Christian South and its people. My central theme is to highlight the desecration committed against schools and colleges, churches and cemeteries. Those were the places where our ancestors studied and were educated. There they worshiped God and there they buried their dead. But to thousands of Federal troops nothing was sacred. I have also included many accounts of desecration and destruction to personal and state property. This helps to explain the extent of widespread havoc and severe damage to all aspects of Southern property and society.

Within the hearts of many Union officers and privates, the burning passion of anti-Southern hatred was raging. Then with many of them, it was the one time chance to live an unrestricted life of crime and lewdness while away from the restraints of their Northern home and family members. With hundreds of Sherman's Bummers, it was a time of excessive consumption of alcohol and prolonged periods of drunkenness that added to the frolic atmosphere while taking their lawless control over a defeated populace. Their sinister deeds would leave scars upon the souls of thousands who suffered, their descendants and even upon Southern society as a whole for generations to come. After the end of the War during the victory celebration parades in Washington D.C., General Sherman, his staff and thousands of these war criminals were hailed as great liberators of the slave race and victors in defeating the Southern white rebels. Sherman himself was given the respect and recognition equal only to an ancient conquering king. Many U.S. military officers were promoted to higher rank and given other assignments such as subduing the Indians of the West. Many officers became prominent businessmen, government bureaucrats and even United States presidents, such as James A. Garfield and Benjamin Harrison. The famed Ulysses S. Grant was popularly elected on his record as a military hero in spite of his known prolonged binges of drunkenness, his administrative ineptitude and moral weakness. It is frightening to consider that many of these U.S. federal officers that allowed, even encouraged, the thievery and destruction and perhaps personally participated in these villainous acts of violence became 'national leaders' for the next forty years. It is known that many of the high ranking officers were recipients of expensive stolen valuables, such as gold, silver, jewelry and household items.

In reflection upon the post-war era of American history and the lack of personal integrity and moral quality on the part of our national leadership, it reminds us of the following maxim; "When small men cast long shadows, you know the sun is about to set."

No doubt there were multiplied hundreds of incidences of Northern brutality of non-military necessity committed that went unrecorded. The recorded acts are just a fraction of an unknown total, yet finding those recorded incidences is a major task. So my search goes on even after the printing of this volume. Therefore, this is an on-going story and an unfinished task.

Note to the reader: If by chance you have a book, diary, document or any substantiated record of Northern desecration upon these Southern institutions, I would greatly appreciate you passing them my way. Also welcomed are stories passed down from the old-timers by word of mouth that I can later put into writing. This would greatly be appreciated and acknowledged in any future updated printing.

Until the day when all wrongs are made right by our Holy and Sovereign God - the *Master Record Keeper* of the deeds of all men of all time - read and weep!

Note: Misspelled words in quotes copied from various sources are intentionally left uncorrected and allowed to remain as found in the original text.

Charles A. Jennings
January 31, 2001

A SOLEMN WARNING

"I have said I do not dread industrial corporations as instruments of power to destroy this country, because there are a thousand agencies which can regulate, restrain and control them; but there is a corporation we may all dread. That corporation is the federal government. From the aggressions of this corporation, there can be no safety, if it is allowed to go beyond the well defined limits of it's powers. I dread nothing so much as the exercise of ungranted and doubtful powers by the government. It is, in my opinion, the danger of dangers to the future of this country. Let us be sure to keep it always within it's limits. If this great, ambitious, ever growing corporation becomes oppressive, who shall check it? If it becomes too wayward who shall control it? If it becomes unjust, who shall trust it? As sentinels of the country's watchtower, Senators, I beseech you to watch and guard with sleepless dread, that corporation which can make all property and rights, all states and people, all liberty and hope it's plaything in an hour, and it's victims forever."

Benjamin H. Hill March 27, 1878.
(1823-1882) U.S. Representative, U.S. Senator and a Confederate senator from the state of Georgia

"The Constitution is not an instrument for the government to restrain the people; it is an instrument for the people to restrain the government – lest it come to dominate our lives and interest". . .
-Patrick Henry-

SOUTHERN CULTURE
and
NORTHERN HATRED

Although hundreds of volumes have been written to recount the heinous events that took place during the War for Southern Independence, it is imperative to again remind ourselves of those dreadful years. This present generation needs to catch a glimpse of the horror, devastation, fear and every imaginable form of loss that was suffered by the Southern people. Even to this day, over 135 years later, the proud descendants of those brave Southerners of the mid-nineteenth century are made to feel the blame and shame for causing the worst event in American history. The distortions and outright lies that are still told as to the causes of that war are not only appalling but are also expressed in a most hateful, mean-spirited demeanor. The same attitude that was expressed by the fanatical abolitionists and radical republicans preceding and during the 1860's is still alive and well in our land today. Today's native Southerner is not even given a fair chance to voice his or her opinion because of the loud and over-bearing cry and obnoxious attitude of the self-proclaimed liberal elite. In any discussion concerning the historical North/South conflict which resulted in the so-called Civil War, **the rhetoric of the victor has always been louder than the logic of the loser!**

The causes for which the average Southern soldier fought can be summarized into three distinct yet interwoven principles: Southern culture, Biblical Christianity and constitutional government. Concerning the latter, General Robert E. Lee stated:

"All that the South has ever desired was the Union as established by our forefathers should be preserved and that the government as originally organized should be administered in purity and truth."

In essence, the South fought to preserve its way of life. One blatant fact to keep in mind is that **the South was invaded and the North was the aggressor.**

In the old ante-bellum South, the people possessed a unique and distinct way of life that was a result of several contributing factors. Mainly, their ancestral culture of Celtic background, an abiding religious faith expressed in traditional Protestant Christianity, produced a strong sense of regional loyalty and a tenacious devotion to family and friends. Even though these same traits could be found among many Northerners, the thing that was so unique in the South is that these traits were widespread and, therefore, were principles that shaped Southern society as a whole. Coupled with the fact that the South was basically an agrarian society which made for a very pleasant and peaceful lifestyle, it is easy to understand why the Southern people, both soldier and civilian, fought so desperately to preserve their way of life. Without doubt, when the Southern male left his home to go to the battlefront, he went with a deep sense of personal pride, devotion and honor to defend his farm, home and fireside, family, cultural and religious values by which he lived.

Even in the face of overwhelming odds, the thought

of surrender was not in the Southern soldier's mind. Finally, (after four arduous years of fighting) surrender was considered in order to prevent further bloodshed and devastation. After enduring the type of total war, which was sometimes expressed in savagery and barbarism, by the invading Union armies, the South knew well that defeat would be as cruel as the war itself. Confederate General Patrick Cleburne aptly expressed what defeat would mean to many Southern future generations when he said;

"Surrender means that the history of this heroic struggle will be written by the enemy; that our youth will be trained by Northern school teachers; learn from Northern school books their version of the war; and taught to regard our gallant dead as traitors and our maimed veterans as fit subjects of derision."

Possibly, one of the reasons why so many Union troops took personal liberty, sometimes with the consent or even under the order of a commanding officer, to desecrate Southern houses of worship was because of the widespread support of Southern churches for secession and the cause of the war. Throughout the war, many churches and prominent local and denominational leaders worked diligently to raise and maintain public morale by preaching fiery sermons that contained a mixture of both religious and patriotic fervor. Some church congregations went so far as to donate their church bell to the War Department to be cast into a cannon, while others sent cash offerings to the Confederate Treasury in Richmond to help defray the war effort. It was a common practice indeed for pastors, evangelists and religious leaders of all denominations to offer up public prayers invoking the help of the Lord of Hosts to assist the Confederate cause to total victory and to defeat the evil designs of their enemies.

Throughout the course of the war, many sermons contained the admonitions and inspiring declarations that the cause of Southern independence was not only the will of God, but also in defense of His Supremacy. The general religious consensus of Southern society at the time was an overwhelming Protestant Christianity of a conservative evangelical nature. This stood in blatant opposition to the liberal socialized so-called gospel of the more prominent churches of the religiously 'progressive' North. By the 1850's, the once Bible-based Reformed theology of the Pilgrim Fathers in most New England churches had been cast aside in favor of Unitarianism and Romanticism. This atmosphere of religious, social and intellectual liberalism coupled with the rabid hatred of radical abolitionism served as the Union soldiers' justification to inflict as much pain as possible upon the people and institutions of the South. The South with its beliefs and practices in the 'ole time religion' and Victorian social values was looked upon as a sectional stigma to the many 'enlightened' elitists of the industrialized North.

In spite of the strong religious influence of the many Christian churches and ministers, the general morale and spiritual fervor began to decline in the South during the last half of the war. The factors responsible for this condition were a combination of circumstances from both within and without the Confederate states. Commenting on the religious disruption and negative affects upon Southern church life caused by the war, Bell Irvin Wiley in his Embattled Confederates (pp. 194-195) gives the following description of the impact of the brutal federal invasion into the private lives of Confederate citizens.

Approach of the Federal armies disrupted church services and caused congregations to dwindle. "The ways of Zion languish and mourn," *The Synod of Mississippi*

Reported in the Fall of 1863. "Pastors are parted from their flocks, God's worship interrupted or forbidden, while from many churches God's people are exiled sheep, scattered without their shepherds, the remnants left behind either worshiping in secret, or listening in their sanctuaries to strangers whose voices they do not know and whom they cannot follow." At Vicksburg, Fredericksburg, Atlanta and elsewhere churches were damaged by shells or destroyed by fire. In its minutes for 1864, the Dover Baptist Association of Virginia stated: "The commodious edifice of one of our largest churches is now a heap of ruins. Another building pierced by the cannon balls of our invaders shows ghastly rents ... seven of our churches are within the enemy's line ... their members refugees." In a few instances congregations were subjected to Federal fire in the midst of their worship. On June 23, 1863, Father Lawrence W. O'Bannan of Vicksburg, Mississippi, wrote in his diary: "Mr. Donovan's arm shot off this morning in front of the church by a parrott shell from the point. When I was about to go on the altar another shell passed through the church (but) no one hurt."

In July, 1864, General Robert E. Lee wrote his wife: "The shells have scattered the poor inhabitants in Petersburg so that many churches are closed, indeed they have been visited by the enemy's shells ... Mr. Platt, pastor of the principal E(piscopal) church ... held service again today under the trees near my camp. We had quite a large congregation ... During the service I constantly heard the shells crashing among the houses in Petersburg."

Some ministers abandoned their flocks rather than submit to Federal control. Others experienced misfortunes which severely curtailed their spiritual activities. A Georgia woman noted in her journal during Sherman's invasion: "No church, our preacher's horse stolen by the Yankees."

Mrs. Susan P. Mills of Louisiana wrote her daughter in September, 1864: "Our preacher was taken prisoner above Clinton and was robbed of his fine mare, his buggy and clothes and even his ordination papers. There was a contribution made up yesterday for him and I hope he will soon be able to buy another horse."

Both Confederates and Federals converted churches into hospitals. Union soldiers occasionally were billeted in houses of worship; in some instances they mutilated furnishings, used benches for firewood and did other damage to the premises. The invaders took over the conduct of services in some churches. But usually they permitted the regular minister to continue preaching provided no "disloyal" sentiments were injected into sermons or prayers. Worshipers, too, were expected to take cognizance of the new order. Five Vicksburg ladies who stalked out of an Episcopal church on Christmas Day, 1863, when the "loyal" minister prayed for the President of the United States were banished from the city and sent beyond the Union lines.

> *"If it costs ten years, and ten to recover the general prosperity, the destruction of the South is worth so much."*
> *Ralph Waldo Emerson*

During 1863-1865 in both invaded and uninvaded areas, the growing pinch of war took its toll of religious activities. Synods, conferences and other church gatherings met irregularly, if at all. Many church papers had to suspend publication. Numerous ministers had to seek other employment because their pay would not support their families. Clergymen vacating their positions for any reason were difficult to replace, for the Confederacy, while not subjecting ordained ministers to conscription, made no provision for exempting theological candidates. The result was a sharp decline in the number of persons seeking ordination. In 1858 new preachers admitted to the Georgia Methodist Conference totaled 27; in 1861, the number was 10; in 1862, 6; and in 1864, only 3.

St. John's Church

This was one of many historic churches located in the beautiful city of Richmond, Virginia. It is believed that this is the church where Patrick Henry gave his famous "Give me Liberty" speech in 1775.

Christ Church in Alexandria, Virginia

This was one of the many churches that played an important part in the religious life of the old South.

(Taken from *The Embattled Confederacy* Vol. 3 of *The Image of War 1861-1865*, National Historical Society 1982.)

TOTAL WAR IN THE
SHENANDOAH VALLEY

The original intent of many fanatical abolitionists, radical republicans, the Lincoln administration, the political, journalistic and religious establishment of the North in their psychological and military assault upon the South, was to so permanently change the totality of Southern culture, politics and religion so that it would never be the same again. This rabid hatred of the South was transferred to and instilled in many Union Army generals and troops which they expressed in their military plans which they called 'Total War.' Union General Philip H. Sheridan expressed his contempt and seething hatred for the people of Virginia when he said that it was his intention to wreak such devastation in the Shenandoah Valley that "a crow flying over would have to carry his own rations."

Seemingly, he was a man who had no sense of humane regard for his fellowman. The true nature of this warmonger and his crimes are reported in the Southern Historical Society Papers, Vol. 29, 1901. This officer is reputed to have said that the true principles for conducting war are - *"First. Deal as hard blows to the enemy's soldiers as possible, and then cause so much suffering to the inhabitants of the country that they will long for peace and press their government to make it. Nothing should be left to the people but eyes to lament the war."* In Sheridan's letter to Grant, dated Woodstock, October 7, 1864, he says of his work: *"In moving back to this point the whole country, from the Blue Ridge to the North Mountain, has been made untenable for the rebel army. I have destroyed over 2,000 barns filled with wheat and hay and farming implements; over 70 mills filled with flour and wheat; have driven in front of the army over 4,000 head of stock, and have killed and issued to the troops not less than 3,000 sheep. This destruction embraces the Luray Valley and Little Fort Valley, as well as the Main Valley.*

A large number of horses have been obtained, a proper estimate of which I cannot now make.

Lieutenant John R. Meigs, my engineer officer, was murdered beyond Harrisonburg, near Dayton. For this atrocious act all the houses within an area of five miles were burned."

"It is not generally known, we believe, that this policy of devastation on the part of Sheridan was directly inspired and ordered by General Grant, who, in his Memoirs, writes with great satisfaction and levity of the outrages committed by Sherman, before referred to, and which he, of course, understood would be committed, from the terms of Sherman's telegram to him, and which he, at the last, acquiesced in.

"On the 5th of August, 1864, he (Grant) wrote to General David Hunter, who preceded Sheridan in command of the Valley, as follows, viz: *"In pushing up the Shenandoah Valley, where it is expected you will have to go first or last, it is desirable that nothing should be left to invite the enemy to return. Take all provisions, forage and stock wanted for the use of your command; such as cannot be consumed destroy."*

On another occasion Grant wrote to Sheridan and said, "If the war is to last another year, we want the

Shenandoah Valley to remain a barren waste." *From The Shenandoah Valley of Virginia 1861-1865 A War Story by Sanford C. Kellogg 1903.*

This was nothing more than wanton destruction and vandalism under the guise of war. It was utter devastation and malicious thievery committed by ruthless men under orders from their high command as a way for them to vent their vile feelings of hate and contempt upon helpless civilians. Besides committing outright thievery from personal residences, depleting the inventories of stores and abusing any Southerner at will, their willful disregard for sacred houses of worship and cemeteries was appalling even to some of their own soldiers. Recorded in *William Wallace's Civil War Letters: The Virginia Campaign*, edited by John O. Holzhueter, stored in the Milwaukee Historical Society, is an entry by 31 year old William Wallace of Banks Division, Wisconsin Regiment.

After all was settled the wagons was sent to Bolliver for our knap sacks and in the meantime we were quartered in the several churches through the town. It was blowing a perfect gale - cold and piercing. No person would open the church we were sent to. The Major ordered two men to break open the door if the old preacher would not open it. In a few minutes he gave up the key, and we were in the Episcopal Church. At 4 in the evening the wagons got back after night, and then we had to go out in the dark and serch for our knap sacks which was not an easy mater to find, but we got them. Made our bed in the pews of the church. It was a curious sight to see so many warlike men in it, the house of the Living God where His Word has often been preached. I felt myself that I was committing a sacralige; but it could not be avoided. The exingences of the time required it, for we could not lay out. The aisles and pews were well carpeted but they were not long that collor with the mud and tobacco spit. At this moment it is rediculous to look at, but the boys says it is owned by rebels and it is no harm. They hardly ever stop playing the organ, while others is playing cards and playing the fiddle and dancing, swearing all around. This war will ruin many a soul. It is handing it over to Satan each day.

Some of the companies has their tents in the cemetary with the head of the living against the headstone of the dead. The toomstones serves for tables to eat off, and at the same time blaspheming the name of the Redeemer, not thinking how soon they may be in the Land of Forgetfullness."

Typical of the Union Army under the command of Sheridan in the Shenandoah were widespread reports of pillage and looting, which Sheridan referred to as 'foraging.' In *Sheridan - The Life and Wars of Gen. Phil Sheridan* (pp. 178-179) by Ray Morris, Jr. he recounts the following incident. 'But the crowning blow came when Wilson showed Sheridan a dispatch from Meade demanding that Wilson defend himself from sensational charges made by the Richmond newspapers that Union cavalry had broken into churches and homes during the raid and that Wilson himself, "a highwayman, a wine-bibber and a modern Sardanapalus," had encouraged such looting.'

"D--n him," Sheridan said of Meade.
"Give him h–l."

Wilson then proceeded to defend his men, although he was forced to concede that "there exists in our cavalry service an organized band of thieves, who are under no restraint whatever, and who have been skillful enough so far to elude every attempt to arrest."

This evil and blatant disregard for sacred houses of worship was not a late development in the war as a result of revenge from weary and war-hardened soldiers. As early as June 1861, Confederate Lieutenant Daniel H. Hill and his men had discovered where the enemy had defaced Bethel Church near Jamestown, Virginia. The evacuating Yankee troops had scrawled on the church walls "Death to the Traitors" and "Down with the Rebels."

Union surgeons performing amputations on wounded Federal soldiers in Middletown's Episcopal Church (VA).

The Shenandoah in Flames by Thomas A. Lewis and the Editors of Time-Life Books, The Valley Campaign of 1864, Time-Life Books, Alexandria, Virginia, 1987

Wilderness Church
(Located in the Shenandoah Valley, VA)

This was the scene of a battle between General Stonewall Jackson and Howard's 11th Corps U.S.A. Notice the riddled roof of this humble meeting-house.

From: Photographic History of the Civil War Vol. 2, Francis T. Miller, Editor in Chief

This sacred House of Worship in Hampton, Virginia, the oldest Protestant church in America, was reduced to an empty and hollow shell.

(Taken from The Embattled Confederacy Vol. 3 of The Image of War 1861-1865, The National Historical Society 1982.)

The interior walls of a church in Falls Church, VA became a convenient place for Union soldiers to desecrate by listing the names of Federal regiments that passed by. Notice the damage that was done to the floor.

More graffiti marks the walls of this House of Worship in Falls Church, VA. These markings were made by soldiers of the 141st Regiment of New York.

(Taken from <u>Fighting For Time</u> of The Image of War 1861-1865 Vol. 4, National Historical Society 1983, p. 116.)

One of the beautiful church buildings of Fredericksburg,
Virginia bears the battle scars of the Union's military
invasion of the South.

*(Taken from <u>The Embattled Confederacy</u> Vol. 3 of The
Image of War 1861-1865, the National Historical Society
1982.)*

The Massaponax Church in Virginia was used as General Grant's temporary Field Headquarters. At Grant's order, the pews were moved outside the church so they could be used in an open air Council of War.

(Taken from <u>The South Besieged</u> Vol. 5 of The Image of War 1861-1865, the National Historical Society, 1983.)

Union General U.S. Grant and his staff holding their open-air Council of War sitting on the pews that they had removed from Massaponax Church.

(The South Besieged, Vol. 5)

TOTAL WAR IN THE DEEP SOUTH

In recounting the story of waste and devastation under the command of Union General W. T. Sherman is only a repeat of what took place under General Sheridan, except it was much worse. In Sherman's siege of the city of Atlanta and his subsequent march to the sea, his stated intention was to "break the back of the South." In his official report concerning his military campaign through the heart of the South, he alluded to the demolition of five railroads which served as the Confederacy's major means of transporting food and military supplies to its armies. In his own words Sherman said:

"We have also consumed the corn and fodder in the region of country thirty miles on either side of a line from Atlanta to Savannah, as also the sweet potatoes, cattle, hogs, sheep and poultry, and have carried away more than ten thousand horses and mules, as well as a countless number of their slaves. I estimate the damage done to the state of Georgia and its military resources at one hundred millions of dollars; at least twenty millions of which have inured to our advantage, and the remainder is simple waste and destruction. This may seem a hard species of warfare, but it brings the sad realities of war home to those who have been directly or indirectly instrumental in involving us in its attendant calamities".

(From: The Siege of Savannah in December 1864 and The Operations in Georgia and The Third Military District of South Carolina During General Sherman's March From

Atlanta to the Sea by Charles C. Jones, Jr. 1874)

Midway Church in Midway, Georgia

Sherman vandalized the church, and used it for a
slaughterhouse.

Horse in church

A Solitary Union Scout

"Corporal James Pike, of the Fourth Ohio Cavalry, was already most favorably known to his superior officers by his scouting services, when, early in April 1862, he was dispatched by Gen. Mitchel to Decatur Alabama, to gather information regarding the strength of the enemy, and if possible, to destroy the railroad bridge at that point. He went alone, as he would thus be liable to less suspicion, and would be better able to escape, if pursued, than if accompanied by a small force; while a large one was, of course, out of the question.

". . . he came to a small country church. It was Sunday, and the congregation was devoutly listening to the sermon; but in that congregation there might be Confederate soldiers. Determined, like a prudent general. To leave no enemy in his rear, and yet knowing that it might be dangerous to dismount in order to investigate, he spurred his horse up the two or three steps that the floor of the building was raised above the ground, right into the middle and only aisle. As the horse's hoofs struck loudly upon the floor, the congregation started from its attitude of rapt attention, the preacher, whose hand was raised and in the act of coming down with a thump upon the pulpit, paused in the sermon and the gesture, to look at the singular spectacle of an armed horseman in a church.

"Sorry to interrupt you, sir," he said, addressing the preacher; "are there any Southern soldiers in the church!"

"I-I believe not, sir," replied the startled divine, turning his eyes instinctively to the back door, which stood open.

"Suspecting that there had been Southern soldiers in the building a few moments ago, and that the back door had been their means of exit, he directed the preacher to offer a prayer for the President of the United States, backed his horse out of the building, and rode on, realizing that in rapid movement was his only safety from an aroused country, and saw that he had already disturbed the worshipers only too completely."

Deeds of Daring by Both Blue and Gray by D. M. Kelsey, J. L. Hebert Publishing Co. 1887, pp. 139, 142, 143

Sherman's Bummers

"A raider on his own account - a man who temporarily deserts his place in the ranks while the Army is on the march, and starts out upon an independent foraging expedition. Sometimes he is absent for a few days only, occasionally he disappears for weeks together."

Captain George W. Nichols
Aide-de-Camp to General Sherman

****

"A dirty, ragged man, with his face smoked by many pine-knot fires, riding a stolen mule or horse far on the flanks of the marching columns."

Pepper & Conyngham - Union Staff Officers

****

"Think how you would admire him if you were a lone woman, with a family of small children, far from help, when he blandly inquired where you kept your valuables. Think how you would smile when he pried open your chests with his bayonet, or knocked to pieces your tables, pianos, and chairs: Tore your bed clothing in three inch strips, and scattered the strips about the yard . . . Color is no protection from these rough-riders. They go through a Negro cabin in search of diamonds and gold watches with just as much freedom and vivacity as they "loot" the dwelling of a wealthy planter . . . some of them are loaded down with silverware, gold coin and other valuables. I hazard nothing in saying that three-fifths (in value) of the personal property of the country we passed through was taken."

Captain Conyngham - U.S.A.

From: *Merchant of Terror* by John B. Walters

After General Sherman and his Army left western Tennessee in 1864 on his way to Atlanta, Georgia he passed through the state of Mississippi. While in the city of Jackson, many of his troops set about to terrorize the citizens and commit acts of crime from thievery to arson. The aroused soldiers entered residences, appropriating whatever appeared to be of value or happened to strike their fancy. Those articles which they could not carry, they broke or trampled underfoot or otherwise damaged. They thrust their bayonets into pictures and knocked out windows and even removed doors from their hinges. An eyewitness described how household furnishings, including beds and costly coverings, were thrown into the streets and burned. Among the private residences wrecked by the soldiers was that of Bishop Green of the Protestant Episcopal Church. His home was noted for its taste and refinement and even more for its fine library of 3,000 volumes. Sherman's soldiers, no respecters of persons, committed it to the flames. "It was a sad sight," stated one who viewed the ruins; "nothing remained of it but broken walls."

On the night of July 18, General Sherman called his generals together for a banquet in the Governor's mansion, while the work of destruction continued unabated throughout the town. The Confederate Hotel was burned, the penitentiary, Green's cotton factory and the Catholic Church. The Mississippi office, together with a block of private buildings, was destroyed. In the case of the newspaper, the soldiers broke the presses and scattered the type in the street. Books were stolen from the Mississippi State Library. Some of these were later returned by General Ewing in 1867.'

October 30, 1863. More burning. General McPherson of the Federal Army made a raid recently to Canton, Miss. with 2000 cavalry. He burned farmhouses, barns, in fact everything that would burn in the line of his march. The women and children driven houseless and homeless out in the pelting rain. Can such brutes be called men?

The Diary entry of a Washington, D.C. resident
From: Merchant of Terror by John B. Walters

From: Merchant of Terror or General Sherman and Total War by John B. Walters 1973

The following account gives a general description of the conditions that existed and the desecration that occurred in Holly Springs, Mississippi and other nearby towns.

As a result of occupation by the Federal army, the Holly Springs Presbyterian Church was severely damaged. In 1871, the Rev. J. N. Craig recorded that 'the Federal Army, when they occupied this town requested the pastor to preach to them in this church basement, on the first Sabbath, and they used it as a stable for their horses on the next Sabbath. It was afterward used, for a time as an Ordinance Store.' Netty Fant Thompson later recorded that, 'The lumber stored in the upper room for finishing the church was used for coffins. A workman who had been engaged to build the church disappeared with some of the building money on his person.' Soldiers used the church for target practice, and marks of stray bullets may be seen in the bricks around the front doors.

No Federal order for the occupation or administration of the churches is preserved, but when Memphis was occupied some months earlier, Gen. Grant had observed that, 'Affairs in this city seem to be in rather bad order, secessionists governing much in their own way. . . .' He therefore told his commander: 'You can compel all clergymen within your lines to omit from their church services any portion you may deem *treasonable*, but you will not compel the insertion or substitution of anything.'

Holly Springs was raided at least sixty times during the war. As in many locales, churches were singled out for desecration, not because these buildings provided facilities suitable for military use, but their profanation contributed to the discouragement of the hostile populace, perhaps shortening the war.

In Holly Springs, the Episcopal Church was desecrated in a manner similar to the Presbyterian Church, and the Roman Catholic Church was also abused by the soldiers. The Baptist Church was taken over for a hospital. The Methodist Church, while not desecrated, was used as a courtroom, after the accidental burning of the courthouse on the square. Sometime during the war, a Federal soldier from Minnesota took a Bible belonging to the Methodist church, which was returned in 1958 by his descendants. At LaGrange, Tennessee, pews of the beautiful Immanuel Church (Episcopal), revered as the mother church of West Tennessee, were used to make coffins for Union soldiers. At Bolivar, Tennessee, while Gen. Lew Wallace, author of *Ben Hur*, was stationed nearby, he and other Union soldiers worshiped in the Presbyterian Church, which was later taken over for a hospital. If regular services were maintained in the churches, the prayers of the people must have been said under very trying conditions.

In Memphis, Grant's soldiers seized the First Presbyterian Church and nailed the Stars and Stripes over the front, preventing the congregation from meeting. Federals stabled horses in the Chelsea Avenue Presbyterian Church, and Second Presbyterian Church was seized on the ground that its members were disloyal to the Federal government, having sent their church bell to the Confederates to be melted for a cannon.

In some places, Presbyterian churches were put to the torch. The church at Panola (Batesville), Mississippi, was burned. (Members later appealed to Congress for reparations.) At College Hill, near Oxford, soldiers occupied the church and would not permit the congregation to worship; however, when the chaplain held services for the troops, he put away the songbooks for fear that his men would abuse them. In Oxford, where the Union soldiers camped in the yard of the First Presbyterian Church, an attempt was made to burn the building, but Mrs. Henry Rascoe dashed from her house and put out the fire while the soldiers jeered.

Many looked to their own sin as the cause of these desecrations. The annual narrative of religion for the College Hill Church for 1863 called Gen. William Tecumseh Sherman, 'the chastening rod' of an avenging God. The church estimated the losses incurred by its members at $200,000.

The Confederacy had put a million of its men into uniform (out of a total white population of around five million); more than a fourth of these never returned. The North lost heavily in human lives, but the South's loss, proportionate to its population, was four times as great. Of the southern states, Mississippi and Virginia saw the most raids and battles — Virginia had more than three hundred engagements — Mississippi a few less; consequently, these two states suffered the most damage and loss of life.

Presbyterian churches across the South lay in ruins, with pulpits vacant and flocks dispersed. One Georgia presbytery reported that every house of worship in its bounds had been damaged or destroyed. No semblance of regular worship had been maintained in many communities, and the denomination's seminaries were closed for lack of students. To make matters worse, both Union Seminary in Virginia and Columbia Seminary in South Carolina had invested their endowments in

39

Confederate bonds. Only one student reported for classes at Union in January 1864."

The above quote was taken from the book, *Shadow of a Mighty Rock, A Social and Cultural History of Presbyterianism in Marshall County, Mississippi* by Robert Milton Winter, pp. 179-182, 191 & 192.

In his book, Mr. Winter gives an additional account of the total destruction of LaGrange College of Tennessee and the Federal authority's attempt to demand the total allegiance of Southern clergy to the Union.

John N. Waddel, professor in the synodical college at LaGrange, Tennessee, twenty-four miles northeast of Holly Springs (and teacher of Dr. Paine's son Henry) gave this account of the occupation of his home by Federal soldiers and the attempt to silence his preaching:

LaGrange was visited on some three or four different occasions by raiding parties, but it was not permanently occupied until toward the close of the year 1862, when after the fall of Corinth the Northern army was massed in heavy force on the Memphis and Charleston R.R., covering a stretch of country some ten miles in length, and even more planting themselves in force at various points, to the terror and distress of the inhabitants. The town from that time was never free from a garrison, more or less numerous and troublesome, until the close of the war. I remained in the place with my family, consisting of my two daughters and my youngest boy, (the elder son, George, having volunteered just after the fall of

Fort Donaldson,) and I was subjected to very great aggravations and annoyances. I was forced to give up my house as the head-quarters of the notorious Gen. John A. Logan, who allowed me two back rooms for my own use, and another for my daughters, while he occupied the parlor for his own use, and my study was the office of his chief of staff. . . . He remained there three weeks, and while he did not subject me to any insult or outrage, yet he and his aide kept the house and the yard crowded with squads of private soldiers by day, and they were frequently engaged in Bacchanalian revels at night. The consequence of all this was that when the General with his troops evacuated the premises, the rooms occupied by them presented the appearance of having been occupied by any class of tenants but that of gentlemen. . . . The Federal soldiers who were left in LaGrange . . . tore down the College building and used the bricks to build huts, and chimneys to their tents, until there was hardly a vestige left, or trace of the LaGrange College to indicate the spot where it once stood.

Waddel remarks: "With this ends the story of LaGrange College." He adds, "On a certain Saturday morning, as I was seated in my room, I had placed in my hands by an orderly a communication from [the] Provost-marshal, who was in command at that time in LaGrange:

Dec. 13, 1862,

Rev. J. N. Waddel,

Sir: Until you have identified yourself as a citizen of the United States, by renewing your allegiance to the government and constitution thereof, you will discontinue your labors as a minister of the gospel in this place. You have hitherto used all the means in your power to aid this wicked rebellion, and your labors have been successful in creating suffering and death amid a once happy people. Instead of being a humble follower of our Saviour, endeavoring to save a dying world from their sins, you have stirred dissensions, created estrangements in families, and urged vile treason toward the best government that God ever created upon earth. . . . I trust you have seen the error of your ways, and that you will acknowledge the justice of these plain-spoken words.

Respectfully, your obedient servant,
F. F. Peats, Major and Provost-Marshal

"The soldiers had attended the Presbyterian church at LaGrange in large crowds, and Waddel determined that the authorities planned to compel the oath-taking publicly or to arrest him before the congregation, so that he declined to conduct divine service the following Sunday."

(Taken from the book *Shadow of a Mighty Rock*, p. 181)

In the town of Brandon, Mississippi soldiers, who met no resistance, reduced the Methodist Church to a pile of ashes along with the Post Office and government stables.

Suffering the same deplorable fate as Brandon at the hands of unscrupulous Union cavalry were many other once quiet Mississippi towns. Public buildings, businesses and private residences in Enterprise, Quitman, Hillsboro, Bolton, Lauderdale and Canton were pilfered, vandalized or reduced to ashes by use of the torch. In the eyes of these morally depraved, unrestrained, hate-filled terrorists no Southern property or person was considered sacred or deserved the least amount of human respect.

When passing through the state of Mississippi, Sherman and the bulk of his army had proven themselves to be nothing less than devils in human form. In spite of their previous deeds of villainy, they had reserved the worst expression of their deep-seated hostility for the people of Georgia and South Carolina.

> "To secure the safety of the navigation of the Mississippi, I would slay millions – on that point I am not only insane, but mad."
>
> In a letter written from Nashville to General John A. Logan in December 1863 by General W. T. Sherman

It would be nigh to impossible to list all the sinister acts of desecration carried out toward Southern sacred houses of worship and the resting places of the dead during the North's brutal aggressive invasion of The Deep South. From a paper entitled _"Indian Creek Baptist Church"_ written for and at the request of the DeKalb County (GA) Historical Society, Elizabeth Austin Ford in 1950 wrote the following:

"A building was erected at the junction of what is now Memorial Drive and Indian Creek Drive. What this building was like is not now known. It had a short life; when Sherman marched his Yankees into

DeKalb County, they burned the little structure. Services were then discontinued until after the war."

According to an entry in <u>A History of Washington County, Georgia 1784-1989</u> published by The Washington County Historical Society is recorded the fate of one of its local churches. Concerning what later became Davisboro Baptist Church, the entry reads ... *"The house had in 1810 been moved lower down on Williamson's Swamp, and changed its name from Nelson's Meeting House to Jordan's Meeting House. Jordan's Meeting House continued to be active until the Civil War years. In 1864 the church building was partially destroyed by Sherman's men."* This church building was fortunate compared to many others which were totally dismantled or reduced to ashes.

When the Federal Army was forcing its way toward Atlanta in July 1864, they carried out the most unthinkable act of abuse so far in their aggression against the South. Just north of Atlanta, at the town of Roswell were located factories which manufactured cotton and woolen cloth for the Confederate government. Even though noncombatant persons were considered inviolate under the rules of war, Sherman had decided to arrest all factory employees and charge them with treason. General Kenner Garrard's Union cavalry burned the mills and proceeded to round up all the employees in accordance with Sherman's orders. Sherman had written Garrard a letter and said: "I repeat my orders that you arrest all people, male and female, connected with those factories, no matter what the clamor, and let them foot it under guard, to Marietta, where I will send them by cars to the North." In compliance with

Sherman's order, 400-500 employees, mostly women were forced to walk to Marietta, under guard, to be transported by rail to the state of Indiana. It was his intentions that these noncombatants be separated from their husbands, wives, children, friends and loved ones to be removed and placed in strange surroundings far from home.

While enroute to Indiana, these prisoners were confined in an old Seminary building in Nashville, Tennessee. While there, many of the women prisoners suffered cruel abuses by Union troops which were driven by their insatiable and depraved lust. Sherman was informed of these conditions, but showed no compassion toward these innocent citizens whom he considered to be traitors. This unjustifiable act of non-military necessity is a reminder of the ancient heathen conquering kings who deemed their conquered subjects nothing more than human chattel.

After Sherman and his army left the once beautiful city of Atlanta after a night of frolic, pillage and destruction, two hundred acres of the city lay in ashes. Burke Davis in _Sherman's March_ records that, "The only survivors were four hundred houses and a few large buildings, most of them churches. Father Thomas O'Reilly of the Church of the Immaculate Conception, who had assembled a guard of Federal soldiers, saved his church and parsonage and nearby houses - as well as the City Hall and St. Philip's Episcopal, Trinity Methodist, Second Baptist and Central Presbyterian churches.

Atlanta Medical College was saved by another resolute Confederate, Dr. Peter Paul Noel D'Alvigny, a French Army veteran who hoodwinked the enemy. When his last patients were evacuated, Federal soldiers spread straw on the floors of the buildings, ready for the torch. D'Alvigny bribed hospital attendants to pose as patients, and protested to a Federal officer that he must have time to move his wounded.

Thousands of slaves followed the Federal columns in response to the exhortation of the soldiers, only to be abandoned at Savannah.

Many of the soldiers began to attack women in the shadows and out-of-the-way places. Negro women were the most common victims of the bestiality of the troops . . . The bodies of several (Negro) females were found on the morning of Saturday (Feb. 18, 1865), stripped naked and with only such marks of violence upon them as would indicate the most detestable of crimes. . .

From: Merchant of Terror by John B. Walters

"You have no patients. The place is empty, and it burns tonight with the rest of them. Those are my orders."

The doctor led him to an upper room where his hospital attendants lay groaning in a distressing display of helplessness. "All right," the bewildered officer said. "I'll give you until sunrise to get 'em out of here."

The last of the Army was moving out by dawn, and the Medical College survived, overlooked in the haste of departure.

All along the march of Sherman's Army could be heard the prayers and cries of the distressed, the victims of his terror, sporadic gunfire and dying animals. Then suddenly, the sound of a passing army band playing Julia Ward Howe's "The Battle Hymn of the Republic" as the troops joined in this arousing chorus which made for an atmosphere of triumphant revelry and fame.

After the lawless and marauding Union Army had finally left Atlanta and was at a safe distance away, Georgia militia general, W. P. Howard made an inspection tour. Among his assessment of the damages reported to Governor Joseph Brown he stated that "the crowning act" of villainy by Sherman's men, who had broken gravestones in the cemetery, was the dragging of bodies from vaults and replacing them with Federal dead.

The Negro slaves of Georgia who were in the route of Sherman's march faired no better than their white masters. Burke Davis states, "In Sherman's wake, the village of Covington was plundered by a succession of regiments, some of whom preyed upon the slaves themselves. One black girl, a young servant of the Travis family, watching the soldiers pass, recognized some of her clothing in the arms of a soldier and found that her hut had been plundered. Her wails rang out over the noise of passing bands. A German soldier who had forced his way into the house turned to Allis Travis: 'What's de matter wid dat nigger?'"

"Your soldiers," Allie said, "are carrying off everything she owns, and yet you pretend to be fighting for the Negro."

The servant was afraid to speak to the white soldiers, but when she saw a black infantryman wearing her newest hat, she dashed from the yard, shook her fists in his face and shouted, "Oh! If I had the power like I've got the will, I'd tear you to pieces."

This barbarous army continued to loot so that they had more than they could use. They left tons of fresh loot piled along the roadsides to go to waste. Roadsides were littered with corn, fodder, sweet potatoes plus farms contained the rotting flesh of maliciously slain domestic animals.

Located at Frederica, Georgia on St. Simon's Island is the historical Christ Church. It is the second oldest Episcopal Church in Georgia and the third oldest in the nation. During John Wesley's missionary trip to America in the 1740's, he served as the first Protestant minister at Christ Church. Located on the church grounds is the large oak tree under which it is believed he preached. During the war when the Federals took control of the island, troops commandeered the building and nearly destroyed it. The interior and exterior of the building suffered such severe damage that it had to be rebuilt. It was not rebuilt until 1889.

> "The skill and success of the men in collecting forage was one of the features of this march; often I was amused at their strange collections."
>
> **Union General W. T. Sherman**

In November 1864, the Federal troops passed through Milledgeville, Georgia in route to Savannah. While there, they blew up the Confederate arsenal that damaged churches in Capital Square. Previous to the explosion damage, the troops had ruined the church interiors. They had chopped up the pews and used them for firewood and in St. Stephen's Episcopal Church had filled the pipe organ with molasses.

In November 1864, the Federal troops passed through Milledgeville, Georgia in route to Savannah. While there, they blew up the Confederate arsenal that damaged churches in Capital Square. Previous to the explosion damage, the troops had ruined the church interiors. They had chopped up the pews and used them for firewood and in St. Stephen's Episcopal Church had filled the pipe organ with molasses.

Further along their route of terror, they continued to abuse the black population as well as the White. One Negro woman cried in consternation to her master that these Yankees won't even let the dead rest in their graves. She was referring to her small child that she had buried just a week before. The Federals had dug up the child's coffin and left it on top of the ground to be ravished by the hogs.

In their craze for revenge and utter lack of respect for sacred houses of worship, one Federal officer burnt the Sunbury Church near Savannah just simply to send a signal to a U.S. fleet patrolling the coast.

> "I'm going to march to Richmond. I expect to turn north by the end of the month, when the sun does - and when I go through South Carolina it will be one of the most horrible things in the history of the world. The devil himself couldn't restrain my men in that state."
>
> **Union General W. T. Sherman**

The bombarded Graveyard of Central Church at
Charleston, South Carolina

The tombs of the honored ancestors of the citizens
of Charleston lie shattered from the cannonading by the
Federal Army under General Q. A. Gillmore on August 21,
1863.

Not content with sufficient provisions to maintain
the army on their campaign, thousands of Federal troops
engaged in the most atrocious acts of wanton destruction,
knavish thievery and fiendish vandalism that would rival
the nomadic warring tribes of antiquity. "... The Federals
on every hand and at all points indulged in wanton pillage,

wasting and destroying what could not be used. Defenseless women and children and weak old men were not infrequently driven from their homes, their dwellings fired, and these non-combatants subjected to insult and privation. The inhabitants, white and black, were often robbed of their personal effects, were intimidated by threats and temporary confinement, and occasionally were even hung up to the verge of final strangulation to compel a revelation of the places where money, plate and jewelry were buried, or plantation animals concealed. Private residences along the line of march were not exempt from rude search. Articles of value which they contained were carried off at pleasure, and insults continually offered. Corn cribs, emptied of so much of their contents as sufficed to fill the commissary wagons, were often either pulled to pieces or committed to the flames. Cotton houses, gins, screws, and cotton were universally consumed.

Agricultural implements were broken up or carried away, and horses, mules, cattle and hogs were either driven off, or were shot in the fields or uselessly butchered in the pens and lots. Such was the wholesale destruction of this animal life that the whole region stunk with putrefying carcasses, and earth and air were filled with innumerable turkey buzzards battering upon their thickly strewn death feasts. Even churches did not escape the general wreck, their wooden benches, doors and sides being used for camp fires, and their pulpits stripped of their scanty vesture. Grist, flour and sugar mills shared in the common ruin. Labor was sadly disorganized, and the entire region swept by the Federal columns was left in poverty, ruin, demoralization and ashes ... Soldiers often vied with each other in acts of violence, insult, outrage, pillage, desolation and murder." *(From The Siege of Savannah by Charles C. Jones, Jr.)*

After Sherman's marauding army left Savannah, they headed to South Carolina only to repeat their despicable acts of criminality against innocent men, women and children. Before he reached Columbia, he had burned six out of every seven farmhouses on the route of his march. He also burned the towns of Blackville, Graham, Ramberg, Buford's Bridge, Lexington and many smaller towns and hamlets. After his exit from Columbia, many towns and villages served as the object of his fiendish desire as he had torched Allston, Pomaria, Winnsboro, Blackstock, Society Hill, Camden and Cheraw.

Concerning Union desecration in Lancaster, South Carolina, Leland Summers in his *Lancaster News* article dated November 10, 2000, *Ex-Confederates Show Compassion For Foes* gives the following account. "In late January 1865, the Union Army under the command of General William 'Dirty Billy' Sherman entered South Carolina from Georgia after successfully crossing the Savannah and Salkehatchie Rivers ... By the last week of February, Lancaster would fall victim to the 'vicious Yankees' when it would be invaded by Sherman's left flank under the command of General Judson 'Kill'

Kilpatrick. Kilpatrick himself would have a libidinous rendezvous with Union spy Mary Boozer in a home located on Main Street in Lancaster. Eighty percent of the homes in the downtown area were looted and burned. Kilpatrick held disabled soldiers, civilians and children prisoner in the Lancaster County Courthouse. Attempts to burn the courthouse and county jail were foiled by a rainstorm."

"The Lancaster Presbyterian Church on Gay Street was turned into a stable for the Union Cavalry. Pews were overturned and used as feed troughs. Others were chopped up as firewood as soldiers camped in the adjoining cemetery."

The description of the old Lancaster Presbyterian Church according to *Welcome to Lancaster South Carolina 1785 - A Walking Tour For Visitors Guide* gives the following statement. "This first brick church in Lancaster County was erected in 1862. It replaced a wood structure built in 1835 on land purchased from Eliza Gill. The building reflects early Gothic revival style architecture, with 16-inch thick walls of inscribed plaster to resemble stone, hand-molded brickwork around windows. During the War Between the States, Sherman's cavaliers stabled their horses inside the sanctuary." It appears as though the vile debauched men of Sherman's army had no respect whatsoever for houses of worship regardless of their architectural beauty and the dedication of the sanctuary as sacred temples set aside for spiritual worship.

> "The first step in liquidating a people is to erase its memory, destroy its books, its culture, its history . . . Before long the nation will forget what it is and what it was."
>
> Milan Hubl - Historian

A similar fate awaited the Associate Reformed Presbyterian Church of Fairfield County in 1865 at the defiled hands of General Kilpatrick's Union Cavalry. Ebenezer Church as it was often called "was erected in 1788 by the people of the Lower Little River section of the county. They were predominately Scotch-Irish Presbyterians, highly religious, and staunch and fervent in their beliefs ... Near the church there were skirmishes with the Confederates who had the advantage of being located on the ridge. When the Cavalry reached Little River, they found that the Confederates had burned the bridge. In order to avoid the bullets of the sharpshooters in the hills above them, the Yankees took advantage of the little church and ripped out part of the flooring and woodwork to hastily construct a bridge over which they might cross the swollen stream and move on beyond the ridge.

"After they left, a note of apology was found inscribed on some of the woodwork that remained intact. It read thus:

To the Citizens of this county -

Please, excuse us for defacing your house of worship. It was absolutely necessary to effect a crossing over the creek.
(Signed) A Yankee

Occasionally, Union soldiers would show some respect by a small act of 'kindness.' In Boone County, Missouri, soldiers first removed the church's Bible and set it on a stump outside before reducing the church house to ashes.

The Little River Baptist Church, which was erected in 1845 also suffered damage, but to a lesser degree. "The imported prisms of the chandelier were smashed, some of the furnishings abused, and the building left in a general mess" as recorded in *A Fairfield Sketchbook* by Julian S. Bolick located in the Camden, South Carolina Archives.

E. A. Pollard in *The Lost Cause* (1886) records the burning of South Carolina's capitol city in these vivid words. 'In the town of Columbia was a Catholic convent, The Lady Superior of which had educated General Sherman's daughter, and now laid claim to his protection for the young women in her charge. A guard of eight or ten men were detailed for the institution. But a Catholic officer in Sherman's army visited the convent, warned The Lady Superior of danger, and whispered to her, "I must tell you, my sister, Columbia is a doomed city."

'A few moments later, while Mayor Goodwyn was conversing with a Federal soldier, three rockets were shot up by the enemy from the capitol square. As the soldier beheld these rockets, he cried out: "Alas! Alas! For your poor city! It is doomed. Those rockets are the signal. The town is to be fired." In less than twenty minutes after, the flames broke out in twenty distinct quarters.

'Engines and hose were brought out by the firemen, but these were soon driven from their labors – which were indeed idle against such a storm of fire – by the pertinacious hostility of the soldiers; the hose was hewn to pieces, and the firemen, dreading worse usage to themselves, left the field in despair. Meanwhile, the flames spread from side to side, from front to rear, from street to street. All the thoroughfares were quickly crowded with helpless women and children, some in their night clothes. Agonized mothers, seeking their children, all affrighted and terrified, were rushing on all sides from the raging flames and falling houses. Invalids had to be dragged from their beds, and lay exposed to the flames and smoke that swept the streets, or to the cold of the open air in back yards.

'The scene at the convent was a sad one. The flames were fast encompassing the convent, and the sisters, and about sixty terrified young ladies, huddled together on the streets. Some Christian people formed a guard around this agonized group of ladies, and conducted them to Sidney Park. Here they fancied to find security, as but few houses occupied the neighborhood, and these not sufficiently high to lead to apprehension from the flames. But fire-balls were thrown from the heights into the deepest hollows of the park, and the wretched fugitives were forced to scatter, finding their way to other places of retreat, and finding none of them secure ... The best and the most beautiful portion of Columbia lay in ruins. Eighty-four squares of buildings had been destroyed, with scarcely the exception of a single house. The Capitol Building, six churches, eleven banking establishments, the Schools of Learning, the shops of art and trade, of invention and manufacture, shrines equally of religion, benevolence, and industry were all buried together in one congregated ruin.' (Editor Note: **This is not a scene of worn-torn European cities such as Paris, Budapest or Berlin. This happened in America to Americans by Americans.**)

"At an early hour in the day, almost every house

was visited by groups, averaging in number from two to six persons. Some of these entered civilly enough, but pertinaciously entered, in some cases, *begging* for milk, eggs, bread and meat – in most cases, demanding them. In the house, parties less meek of temper than these pushed their way, and the first intimation of their presence, as they were confronted at the entrance, was a pistol clapped at the head or bosom of the owner, whether male or female.

'Your watch!' 'Your money!' was the demand. Frequently, no demand was made. Rarely, indeed, was a word spoken, where the watch or chain, or ring or bracelet, presented itself conspicuously to the eye. It was incontinently plucked away from the neck, breast or bosom. Hundreds of women, still greater numbers of old men, were thus despoiled. The slightest show of resistance provoked violence to the person.

"The venerable Mr. Alfred Huger was thus robbed in the chamber and presence of his family, and in the eyes of an almost dying wife. He offered resistance, and was collared and dispossessed by violence.

"In the open streets the pickpockets were mostly active. A frequent mode of operating was by first asking you the hour. If thoughtless enough to reply, producing the watch or indicating its possession, it was quietly taken from hand or pocket, and transferred to the pocket of the 'other gentleman,' with some such remark as this: 'A pretty little watch that. I'll take it myself; it just suits me.' And the appropriation followed; and if you hinted any dislike to the proceeding, a grasp was taken of your collar, and the muzzle of a revolver put to your ear.

"In several instances parlours, articles of crockery, and even beds, were used by the soldiers as if they were water-closets. In one case, a party used vessels in this way, then put them on the bed, fired at and smashed them to pieces, emptying the filthy contents over the bedding.

"In several cases, newly made graves were opened, the coffins taken out, broken open, in search of buried treasure, and the corpses left exposed. Every spot in graveyard or garden, which seemed to have been recently disturbed, was sounded with sword, or bayonet, or ramrod, in the desperate search after spoil."

****

A lady spoke indignantly to General Atkins, of Sherman's army, and said of that General, "He wars upon women!"

"Yes," said Atkins, "and justly. It is the women of the South who keep up this cursed rebellion. It gave us the greatest satisfaction to see those proud Georgia women begging crumbs from Yankee leavings; and this will soon be the fate of all you Carolina women."

"Escorting a sad procession of fugitives from the burning dwellings, one of the soldiers said:

"What a glorious sight!"

"Terribly so," said one of the ladies.

"Grand!" said he.

"Very pitiful," was the reply.

"The lady added:

"How, as men, you can behold the horrours of this scene, and behold the sufferings of these innocents, without terrible pangs of self-condemnation and self-loathing, it is difficult to conceive."

"We glory in it!" was the answer. "I tell you, madam, that when the people of the North hear of the vengeance we have meted out to your city, there will be one universal shout of rejoicing from man, woman and child, from Maine to Maryland."

From The Lost Cause by E. A. Pollard as reported by the Daily Phoenix

Even though Sherman, and especially his wife, claimed to be of the Roman Catholic faith, he offered no assistance in protecting the property of the Charleston convent. In his book *Sherman's March*, Burke Davis gives this vivid account of the plunder, desecration and final utter destruction of the Roman Catholic convent of Charleston, South Carolina.

'Little more than a mile away, Sister Baptista Lynch had been agonizing over the safety of her convent and its young women and girls. When she heard the first reports of spreading fire and violence across the city, the mother superior had written Sherman once more, a reminder of her "personal as well as religious claim" upon his protection through her acquaintance with Minnie and his sister.

'Sherman responded once more that the convent was in no danger, and that she and her charges should remain where they were.

'It was now too late. The wall of fire advancing through the city raged ever nearer the convent grounds.

Father O'Connell, "looking sad and anxious," came in from the streets to whisper with the nuns, who called the girls aside, helped them to tie clothing into small bundles and gave instructions for evacuating their building. The girls listened gravely. The youngest of them was five, and several were under the age of ten.

'At nightfall, for the first time flames were visible through the convent windows, and the roar of the doomed city's consuming flames could be heard behind the thick walls. The priests tried to remove the Host from the altar, but were dissuaded by the nuns, who wished to keep it as long as possible. Father O'Connell led a final benediction. The schoolgirls were kneeling, reciting the rosary, when the chapel door was broken in by "the most unearthly battering ... like the crash of doom. Drunken soldiers piled over each other, rushing for the sacred gold vessels of the altar, not knowing they were safe in the keeping of one blessed of God."

'The girls filed past the cursing men into the night: "We marched through the blazing streets with the precision of a military band. It was our safety." Father O'Connell led, followed by Sister Baptista. Sara Aldrich, whose mother had sent her here from Barnwell, thought she would remember the scene for life: "Not a cry, not a moan. The roaring of the fires, the scorching flames on either side ... did not create the least disorder. That majestic figure of the Mother Superior in the graceful black habit of the Ursuline order ... The long line of anxious, white young faces of the schoolgirls ..."

'Father O'Connell led them into a nearby church, from which they saw the burning convent roof collapse into a fiery grid of timbers. The sturdy building endured until long after nearby structures had burned to the ground, but at three in the morning its cross plunged earthward in a cascade of flames and embers.

"Laughing soldiers taunted the nuns and blew cigar smoke in their faces. "Oh, holy! We're just as holy as you are! . . . Now, what do you think of God? Ain't Sherman greater?'"

> The Rev. Mr. Connor, a Methodist minister whose parsonage was burned, emerged with a sick child wrapped in a blanket. A soldier seized the blanket. "No!" Connor said, "he's sick." The soldier tore off the blanket and threw it into the fire. "D--n you," he said, "If you say one more word I'll throw the child after it."
>
> Sherman's March by Burke Davis

Besides the acts of violence committed against personal property, the moral behavior of Federal troops sunk to an appalling low degree. Burke Davis, states in his *Our Incredible Civil War* (1960); 'Numerous incidents involving sex and kindred matters were reported during the sack of Columbia, South Carolina, by troops of Sherman. One witness, Dr. D. H. Trezevant, who had much to say of acts of violence in the city, reported on sights in the streets: "It was not unusual to see a Yankee soldier with his arm around the neck of a Negro wench, even in the common thoroughfare, or hugging and kissing a mulatto girl, when he could find one so degraded that she would not spurn him for his impudence and want of common decency!" Davis went on to add the testimony of the novelist, William Gilmore Simms who said: "Negro women, especially in the surrounding countryside, were 'horribly' used. Regiments in successive relays subjected scores of these poor women to the torture of their embraces . . . Horrid narratives of rape are given which we dare not attempt to individualize."

He did write of one Negro woman, raped in Columbia by invading soldiers, who drowned her in a mud puddle. Simms added that Federal troops opened new graves in search of jewels and other valuables, and when they found more horses and mules than they could use, cut their throats.'

The charred remains of the Presbyterian Lecture Room in Charleston, South Carolina.

Old Sheldon Church near Beaufort, SC was originally known as the Church of Prince William's Parish. It was built between 1745 and 1755 and its construction was considered one of the first imitation Greek Temples in America. During the Revolutionary war, British troops burned it in 1779, but was rebuilt in 1826. It was burned again by General Sherman's troops in 1865 and remains in ruins to this day.

Aiken County, South Carolina 1865

James Courtney, was killed by the Yankees in 1865 at the age of fifty-four. This happened during Sherman's March when he was trying to save his home which had been set on fire by Kilpatrick's men. Three times he outened the blaze, only to have his home set afire again. The last time he put the fire out, the Yankees were so enraged that they shot him in the leg as he stood in his yard and left him to bleed to death. As there was no one to treat his wound, he dispatched a servant to a Yankee surgeon for assistance, but the Yankee refused to help and he bled to death. It was thought that the Yankees took revenge on him because he had furnished supplies from his mill to the Confederate Army.

Ninety Years in Aiken County, South Carolina
    By Gasper L. Toole, II

In order to keep warm, Federal troops dismantled every building in sight to be used as firewood in the town of Mareeville, South Carolina.

"Sergeant Fleharty watched as the village church was attacked: "First the pulpit and seats were torn out, then the siding and the blinds were ripped off. Many axes were at work. The corner posts were cut, the building tottered, the beautiful spire, up among the green trees, leaned . . . vibrating to and fro. A tree that stood in the way was cut. By the use of long poles the men increased the vibratory motion of the building, and soon, with a screeching groan the spire sunk down . . . and as the structure became a pile of rubbish, some of the most wicked of the raiders yelled out: 'There goes your damned old gospel shop'"

From: *Sherman's March* by Burke Davis

After the Battle of Aiken, South Carolina, a squad of Confederate General Wheeler's scouts found an old man leaning upon a gatepost sobbing in front of a farmhouse. After an inquiry, the old man, a local Baptist minister, told the scouts in a trembling voice, "My daughter. A bunch of Yankees raped her – They just left here."

According to historian Bill Potter of Charles City, Virginia, "In 1862, Federal troops operating out of Williamsburg, VA, dismantled Liberty Baptist Church in New Kent County to build a bridge across Diascund Creek.

"No battles were fought nearby and no armies were on the move. The area was even undefended at that time. After the war, the surviving church members pulled the bridge apart and reconstructed their church building – The only type of reconstruction tolerated in that place for many years."

HUNGER IN SOUTH CAROLINA

'As the war drew to a close, hunger crept across the Southland. Mrs. G. A. Simpson of South Carolina wrote:

"One of the most interesting things I remember hearing my grandmother tell was about how the country people became so hungry for salt. After Sherman's march of destruction, they dug up the dirt floor in the smokehouse, boiled it, and used the water to cook with. She said she had to ride on the boat from Camden, South Carolina to Charleston to get a peck of meal, the trip taking two days. Rations were issued to the ones that had everything destroyed but they seldom got anything but meal and sometimes a little black molasses. Even their garden seed was destroyed. The people wouldn't plow their gardens the following year, afraid they might cover up some little vegetable plant or seed. They went over the garden with a short handled hoe, looking for and working carefully each little plant that came up."'

From: *True Tales of the South at War*
Collected and Edited by Clarence Poe

Circular Congregational Church was organized in 1681 and was known as The Independent Church of Charles Towne, S.C. The unique circular building was built in 1806. It was severely damaged by fire and Union shelling in 1861 as seen in this 1865 photograph.

From: *Fighting For Time Vol. 4 of The Image of War 1861-1865, the National Historical Society*

In his book, Mr. Davis goes on to record the most degrading and shocking scene of desecration. Union troops engaged in the most vile behavior in their utter disrespect toward both the house of God and the Southern civilian dead.

"The XIV and XX Corps hurried along parallel roads toward Winnsboro, a pleasant village of 2,500 some forty miles north of Columbia. The Reverend W. W. Lord, rector of Christ Episcopal Church, and a four-hundred-pound vestryman who was the local doctor rode from Winnsboro to the Federal camp and begged for the town's protection. They were too late. . . .

"Much of the town, at least thirty houses, went up in flames. The Episcopal Church was burned to the ground after soldiers had removed the organ so that they could play "the devil's tunes" on it. Calling upon the dead to witness the fun, the pranksters dug a coffin from the graveyard, split it with an axe and stood it on end so that its recently dead occupant could take in the ceremony."

It was in Winnsboro where Sherman made a sporadic inspection of the army's trains to find the stolen loot from Columbia. There were five tons of stolen personal and household items that were gathered up and burned. Among the items was a golden figure of Christ, stolen from a Columbia church.

Mr. Davis records more very disturbing acts which proves the contempt toward sacred and holy things on the part of the vain men with hatred toward the Southern people. In Lancaster, some of Sherman's troops came upon another sick boy. This one an eighteen-year-old cadet from The Citadel, a refugee fleeing with his family. Seriously ill with pneumonia, the anonymous boy, together with his family, was surprised by Bummers before the main body of the army reached the town. The boy's mother was kneeling at her morning prayers when the first bluecoat entered and seized her arms from behind.

"Get up, old woman; praying will do you no good now, for Sherman's Bummers are upon you." Soldiers snatched her gold spectacles, emptied her pockets and ransacked her room.

In North Carolina, Sherman's Bummers robbed an Episcopal Bishop, Reverend Thomas Atkinson. They ruthlessly robbed him at gunpoint of his watch, jewelry, clothing and horse.

'After robbing the home of everything of value, the soldiers went down into the cellar, where they "pour kerosene oil, molasses, and feathers together, then stir them up with their bayonets." Such concoctions were usually poured into pianos or spread upon the rugs throughout the house.'

Based upon an eye-witness report at Liberty Hill, S.C.
From: *Merchant of Terror* by John B. Walters

The letter, which is a republication from the Alderson, West Virginia, *Statesman*, of October 29, 1883, is as follows:

"CAMP NEAR CAMDEN, S. C., February 26, 1865

"MY DEAR WIFE:

"I have no time for particulars. We have had a glorious time in this State. *Unrestricted license to burn and plunder was the order of the day.* The chivalry have been stripped of most of their valuables. Gold watches, silver pitchers, cups, spoons, forks, etc., etc., are as common in camp as blackberries. The terms of plunder are as follows: The valuables procured are estimated by companies. Each company is required to exhibit the result of its operations at any given place. *One-fifth and first choice falls to the commander-in-chief and staff, one-fifth to corps commander and staff, one-fifth to field officers, two-fifths to the company.* Officers are not allowed to join in these expeditions, unless disguised as privates. One of our corps commanders borrowed a rough suit of clothes from one of my men, and was successful in his place. He got a large quantity of silver (among other things an old milk pitcher), and a very fine gold watch from a Mr. DeSaussure, of this place (Columbia). DeSaussure is one of the F. F. V.'s of South Carolina, and was made to fork out liberally. Officers over the rank of captain are not made to put their plunder in the estimate for general distribution. This is very unfair, and for that reason, in order to protect themselves, the subordinate officers and privates keep everything back that they can carry about their persons, such as rings, earrings, breastpins, etc., etc., of which, if I live to get home, I have a quart. I am not joking. I have at least a quart of jewelry for you and all the girls, and some No. 1 diamond pins and rings among them. *General Sherman has gold and silver enough to start a bank. His share in gold watches and chains alone at Columbia was two hundred and seventy-five.*

"But I said I could not go into particulars. All the general officers, and many besides, have valuables of every description, down to ladies' pocket handkerchiefs. I have my share of them, too.

"We took gold and silver enough from the d–d rebels to have redeemed their infernal currency twice over. * * * I wish all the jewelry this army has could be carried to the Old Bay State. It would deck her out in glorious style; but, alas! It will be scattered all over the North and Middle States.

"The damned niggers, as a general thing, preferred to stay at home, particularly after they found out that we wanted only the able-bodied men, and, to tell the truth, the youngest and best-looking women. Sometimes we took them off by way of repaying influential secessionists. But a part of these we soon managed to lose, sometimes in crossing rivers, sometimes in other ways. I shall write you again from Wilmington, Goldsboro, or some other place in North Carolina. The order to march has arrived, and I must close hurriedly.

"Love to grandmother and Aunt Charlotte. Take care of yourself and the children. Don't show this letter out of the family.

"Your affectionate husband,

"THOMAS J. MYERS,
"*Lieutenant, etc.*

"P. S. — I will send this by the first flag of truce, to be mailed, unless I have an opportunity of sending it to Hilton Head. Tell Lottie I am saving a pearl bracelet and earrings for her. But Lambert got the necklace and breastpin of the same set. I am trying to trade him out of them. These were taken from the Misses Jamison, daughters of the President of the South Carolina Secession Convention. We found these on our trip through Georgia.

"T. J. M."

"This letter is addressed to Mrs. Thomas J. Myers, Boston, Mass."

This letter was published in the *Southern Historical Society Papers*, in March, 1884.

From: *Southern Historical Society Papers Vol. 29 1901*

The area of South Carolina including Jasper County next to the Georgia state line where it meets the Atlantic Ocean is known as The Lowcountry. It was here, soon after leaving Savannah that Union troops began their barbaric acts of destruction in South Carolina including the desecration of sacred houses of worship and cemeteries.

"Black Swamp Baptist Church was organized in 1781, but its church building was burned by Sherman's troops during the Civil War." *

Gillisonville Baptist Church building was completed in 1838. The steeple was demolished by a Union cannon during the Civil War. Union troops used the church as a headquarters during the war, and one of the old communion plates still used today is inscribed: "War of 1861-2-3-4. Feb. 1865 This done by a Yankee soldier." *

Euhaw Baptist Church was organized in 1751 as part of the Charles Town Baptist Association . . . in 1865 it was destroyed by Union troops. *

Holy Trinity Episcopal Church first began as a congregation in its first chapel in 1829. In April 1830, a larger place of worship was completed and consecrated to the service of God by Bishop Nathaniel Bowen. The present structure was built in 1855 at Grahamville. In late 1864, the church was used as a headquarters for Federal troops and was, therefore, spared destruction by fire. Nearly every other building in Grahamville was reduced to ashes. The church's furnishings were desecrated and looted; even its Bible was carried away. The Holy

Communion silver was saved by a young member who slipped into the church and brought it out. This he did with great risk, because of the presence of Union officers nearby.

In 1928, the stolen church Bible was discovered in the attic of a New York music publisher. The publisher then returned the Bible to the wardens of the church. A Union officer's scribbled name is legible on the flyleaf of the Bible.*

*Source: Jasper County - The Gateway to South Carolina and The Lowcountry Jasper County Chamber of Commerce, Ridgeland, South Carolina

'Churches in all areas which were invaded by Federal forces suffered from desecration and damage of property. Church buildings, equipment, records, and parsonages were often attacked and destroyed. Evidence seems to substantiate the claim that losses of this type were perpetrated by the Federal forces to a degree far exceeding military necessity. An Illinois infantryman, writing about the Federal occupation of Hardeville, South Carolina, said, "Again the work of destroying buildings commenced. A large beautiful church was attacked...the pulpit and seats were torn out, then the siding and blinds ripped off....Many axes were at work...it became a pile of rubbish." In Mississippi the home and library of Protestant Episcopal Bishop William Green were burned by Federal troops after the battle of Jackson. At Holly Springs, Mississippi, and at St. Augustine, Florida, the invaders used the Episcopal churches as stables. The altars were overturned and used as feed troughs. After the battle of Atlanta the basement of the Central Presbyterian Church in that city was used by United States authorities as a slaughterhouse.

'At Fredericksburg, Virginia, Church Hill, Mississippi, and Helena, Arkansas, Northern soldiers played lewd songs on the church organs, danced in the buildings, and stole the silver communion services. Federal troops confiscated the seats, destroyed the pulpit, and "carried off" the window sash of the Baptist Church in Suffolk, Virginia. The Oak Grove Methodist Church in Jackson County, Alabama, was torn down by Federal troops and the materials were used to build a pontoon bridge across the Tennessee River. At Corinth, Mississippi, the Christian Church was torn down and the brick used to construct "chimneys and ovens in the camps of Federal forces." A Methodist church in Shellmound, Tennessee, was used by Federal soldiers as a "shed for horses," and St. Stephen's Lutheran Church in Shenandoah County, Virginia, was destroyed and the materials used to construct a signal tower. Baptist and Methodist church buildings at New Bern, North Carolina, and Charleston, South Carolina, were used as warehouses for the storage of commissary supplies by Federal military authorities. Some church buildings were used by Federal soldiers as targets for rifle and artillery practice, and it was reported that at least one church building was taken over by the Federals and tenated with a group of black women, who were called "wives of United States soldiers."

'Practically all of the church buildings in Pine Bluff, Arkansas, Franklin, Tennessee, and Fredericksburg, Virginia, were damaged or destroyed by United States military authorities during the war, and numerous churches in other areas were torn down and the materials used to construct barracks. It is claimed that in Virginia twenty-six Baptist churches were completely destroyed by Federal troops and that throughout the South, United States personnel destroyed or seriously damaged more than sixty Presbyterian Church buildings. In the Protestant Episcopal Diocese of South Carolina ten church buildings were burned and three others were "wrecked," and eleven parsonages were destroyed by fire. In Knoxville, Tennessee, it was reported that every Methodist church in that city was either destroyed or damaged during the war. In addition to destroying church property, Federal forces and even Confederate authorities converted many church buildings into hospitals for the sick and wounded.'

From: *Southern Protestantism in the Confederacy* by W. Harrison Daniel, 1989

When the Federal forces under Sherman's command finished wreaking havoc in the state of South Carolina, they headed toward North Carolina with somewhat less fury of hatred and evil design. They still vented their unbridled feelings of destruction in several places and one such place was in the town of Wilmington near the Atlantic coast. Below is a description of their abuse and desecration which they committed against St. Paul's Evangelical Lutheran Church.

"In the month of January, 1863, after a severe and protracted struggle, Fort Fisher fell, this gave the Federal troops almost free and easy access to the city; consequently on the 22d day of February following, the city of Wilmington was evacuated by the Confederate soldiers, and occupied by the Northern army, which practically ended the war, so far as the city of Wilmington was concerned. But whilst it terminated to many the duties, privations and hardships of active warfare, it produced new evils that were not experienced during the progress of the war.

"The unfinished Lutheran church edifice was soon occupied by Northern troops, who despoiled it of all that could be taken from and around it, serviceable to light their camp fires, the fencing, the joists in the church, the pews in the lecture room, and its reading desk, were thus destroyed; even the Sunday School library books were taken away, the beautiful tower, as far up as the eye could reach, was blackened like the inside of a chimney with the blaze and smoke of the soldier's campfires, whilst the lecture room was defiled with profane inscriptions upon its walls, and its floors put in such a condition, that the place could not be used again for divine worship, until the whole of it was renewed and remodeled. All this was a sad spectacle to behold, as observed by the writer himself the following year, during one of his visits to the congregation, and presented an illustration of the depravity of man not easily forgotten.

"The Sunday School had now no place of assembly, and no library for the children; it had therefore reluctantly to be abandoned, and with its abandonment seemed to perish, in the hearts of many of the members, the last lingering hope of the Lutheran Church in Wilmington, N. C. This was the darkest period of its existence, at which time some of its leading members advised the selling of the church property, the payment of its debts, and the division of the balance of the money, if there should be any; to the original donors, in proportion to the amounts they had given to this once hopeful enterprise."

The above quote was a first-hand report given by the pastor of the church, G. D. Bernheim, D.D., in his book *The First Twenty Years of the History of St. Paul's Evangelical Lutheran Church*, published in 1879.

In addition to the damage committed to both public and private property in the city of Wilmington, the ruthless control of the occupational forces extended even to their attempt to determine church liturgy. Below is a description of Yankee mistreatment of the pastor of St. James Episcopal Church and their desecration of the church building.

"The years of the War Between The States brought a difficult and dramatic period to St. James Church. In July, 1861, A. J. deRosset was elected as an alternate delegate from the Dioceses of North Carolina to a meeting of the southern dioceses at Columbia, SC. The meeting was called to form a constitution for the Episcopal Church in the Confederate States of America.

"During the first battle of Fort Fisher in December, 1864, the thunder of the guns was heard irregularly during Christmas services at St. James until the Litany was begun, then the responses of the congregation and the roar of guns became united. "From battle and murder and from sudden death," read the minister. "Good Lord, deliver us," prayed the congregation and simultaneously "boom, boom, boom," answered the guns. On January 15, 1865, Fort Fisher was surrendered to the Union forces.

"Bishop Atkinson, on January 27, 1865, authorized "any clergyman within the enemy lines while under the constraint of the enemy, to omit the prayer for the President and Congress of the Confederate States. On February 22, 1865, Wilmington was captured and occupied by the Union forces.

"An order was issued on February 26, 1865, as follows: "Provost Marshal's Office, Lt. J. C. Taggart will procure the keys and take charge of the Episcopal Church of the city immediately and will notify the Rector of the same that they will not be allowed to hold services in the same today. (signed) W. J. Jordan, Lt. Col., 104 Ohio Volunteers, Provost Marshal."

"During this difficult period, more than eighty families belonging to St. James remained in Wilmington.

"After the surrender of Wilmington, Rev. Watson continued to pray for Jefferson Davis, President of the Confederate States of America. General Hawley sent a curt mandate to the rector to discontinue without delay this custom. Rev. Watson replied quickly to the military officer that he had no canonical authority to justify obeying such an order. He said if he should do so he would make himself a party to the infringement of the religious liberty of the Church. Generals Schofield and Hawley filed detailed reports as to this matter. A reply was received that the officers had followed approved procedure in the position they had taken, but if the determined southern minister wished to continue prayers for the Confederate leader, he was to be permitted to do so without further interference or molestation.

"Definite spite against St. James Church was later manifested by General Hawley when the church was seized and converted into a hospital. It was later discovered in old records that the building was never half-filled with patients.

"The pews in the church were ripped out with pick axes and all furnishings were removed by military authority on April 7, 1865. About five days later, Rev. Watson wrote to Abraham Lincoln giving his reasons for not praying for the President of the United States. This letter was never mailed, possibly because Lincoln was assassinated two days later.

"Religious services were resumed in St. James Church in December, 1865, after $613.00 was expended for the necessary repairs to the building. On January 5, 1886, a committee was appointed by the vestry to prepare a bill to be presented to the United States Congress to reimburse the parish for the use and damage to the church building by Union troops in 1865. Instructions were given to the senior warden in May, 1898, to proceed with the claim against the federal government for damages to the church during the occupation of 1865."

The above description is recorded in the *History of St. James Parish, 1729-1979*, by Leora Hiatt McEachern; 1982.

Chris E. Fonvielle, Jr. comments on this same incident by adding that "they punished Watson by closing St. James, suspending the reverend's religious privileges, and threatening to banish him from the district. A few weeks later General Hawley seized the church and a squad of U. S. Colored Troops proceeded to tear out the pews, throw them into Third Street, and transform the house of worship into a military hospital." (*The Wilmington Campaign - Last Days of Departing Hope* by Chris E. Fonvielle, Jr.)

On November 1900, the church vestry of St. James presented the United States government a damage claim for $5,330.00. The amount received from the federal government in March, 1905 was $3,131.00.

"In Burnished Rows of Steel"

17th New York Infantry

Typical scenes as portrayed in these photographs served as the inspiration for Mrs. Julia Ward Howe in composing the lyrics for the now popular song: The Battle Hymn of the Republic. Mrs. Howe, along with her Unitarian pastor, James Freeman Clarke, Massachusetts Governor Andrew, and her husband, Dr. Samuel G. Howe visited the Union Army near Washington, D.C. in the fall of 1861. This so-called hymn became the rallying cry of both the Union Army and civilians in their self-justification for their inhumane and barbaric treatment of the South. It was widely used by the Lincoln administration as a very effective tool of humanistic propaganda in mustering political support and lifting public morale.

"HIS TRUTH IS MARCHING ON"

9th Vermont Infantry

The Battle Hymn of the Republic —
"A Hundred Circling Camps"

In 1861 of the Fifth Vermont camped near Camp Griffin
not far from Washington, D.C.

The Photographic History of the Civil War - The Armies
and Leaders, Poetry and Eloquence, Vol. 5

DIVINE PRESERVATION

In consideration of the many instances of burning, desecration and outright destruction of scores of Southern churches listed in this narrative, it behooves us to remember with praise our Sovereign God's preservation of the city of Charleston, South Carolina. The Republican politicians and the liberal establishment of the North looked upon the city of Charleston as the hot bed of 'secession' and therefore held an utter contempt for its citizens, its philosophical, social and religious influence over the rest of the Confederacy. They determined to rid the country of this menace which was born in the city of Charleston, even if it meant the literal destruction of the whole city and the cruel death of many of its citizens.

Providentially, through the righteous influence of one Presbyterian pastor, Dr. John L. Girardeau, God saw fit to foil the plans of the enemy and to preserve the city from destruction by fire. Dr. Girardeau was not only a pastor, but was truly a man sent from God and a most powerful preacher. His life and pulpit ministry was unusually blessed as he delivered the Word of God to thousands of listeners under the anointing of the Holy Spirit. Under the dynamic preaching of Dr. Girardeau in Charleston in 1858, the citizens of that city witnessed a true heaven-sent revival which resulted in the conversion of hundreds of souls and helped prepare the city to withstand the coming hardships of war.

In his book, "Preachers with Power," Douglas Kelly

relates how God used the influence of Dr. Girardeau and his pulpit ministry to thwart the plans of federal instigators and prevent a most devastating fire.

...Charleston was the citadel of 'Secession,' and as such, detested by the Federal authorities, and most of the people of the North. Not a few of these yearned to see it laid in ashes...Several times efforts were made to secretly organize the negroes, and through them to start fires at the same time in many parts of the city. Special agents were employed to carry out such designs, and more than once they almost succeeded.

After the war it became an open secret why these well laid schemes were frustrated. Some leaders of the negroes religiously believed that Dr. Girardeau was the special representative of God to their race; and his church a holy temple in which the Almighty delighted to dwell. They feared, and they imparted this fear to other leaders, that if negroes burned that city so dear to this man of God, and that church so beloved and honored by the Lord of heaven, then the divine curse might rest upon them and heaven withhold that freedom which they felt was almost within their grasp. The self-sacrificing work of one man indirectly but really saved 'The City by the Sea'.

From: *Preachers with Power* by Douglas F. Kelly, *The Banner of Truth Trust*, 1992 p. 167

CULTURES IN CONFLICT

After reviewing the many despicable and inexcusable acts of violence and terrorism committed against the people of the South, one is left with the haunting questions; Why did they do this? What was their motivating force? And what was their ultimate goal and purpose?

During this time in American history, the mindset of the average citizen of the North had been determined by a long hard-fought battle of political, social and religious propaganda. This campaign of anti-Southern antagonism and often blatant hatred was waged on several simultaneous fronts and aimed at determining not only popular opinion but also shaping political policy and eventually military action. It was only a matter of sixty years or so before the War of 1861-1865 that the general consensus of the North began to drastically change from one of social, political and religious conservatism to one of liberalism and a so-called 'cultural progressivism.' This change was a result of several factors, both foreign and domestic in origin. The major factors which served as a philosophical catalyst were the concepts of the French Revolution which had recently transpired in the 1790's. Many politicians, educators, editors, ministers and other people of influence espoused the ideals and social utopian concepts of the French Revolution and set out to implement them in whole or in part in order to change traditional American cultural values.

Unfortunately, their philosophical successors are still at work in our national, state, local, public and private institutions trying to fine tune the socialist concepts of their cultural revolutionary heroes.

Many prominent Northern poets and writers such as Ralph Waldo Emerson, John Greenleaf Whittier, Henry Wadsworth Longfellow, Julia Ward Howe, Harriet Beecher Stow and many others were very popular proponents of liberal socialism. They were very convincing and therefore molded Northern public opinion through the means of their poems, speeches and popular novels. They championed the cause epitomized in the French Revolution slogan of *Liberté, Equalité and Fraternité*. They were the forerunners of the modern day civil rights and feminist movements.

In addition to politicians and other social reformers, were the so-called 'Christian' ministers who were leading this pack of vicious wolves in their sadistic attack upon Southern culture. While the poets were mainly idealogical romanticists, these ministers were mainly Unitarian in their approach to the Holy Scriptures and spiritual values. Seemingly, it was a large segment of the Northern self-proclaimed intellectual elites of all professions who felt that it was their humanitarian duty to proclaim, for example, a doctrine of equality among the races yet vehemently advocated the utter subjugation of the Southern whites. These Northern radicals fervently hated everything that the South stood for, which was; Constitutional government as originally given by our colonial forefathers; Southern culture which involved a traditional patriarchal oriented, agrarian, freedom-loving lifestyle of Anglo-Saxon Celtic origin; and Biblical Christianity as expressed through the Protestant Reformation.

The epitome of hatred which festered in the hearts

of many Northern social liberals could be summed up in the statement of Henry W. Longfellow. During the War he wrote to a friend and said, "Meanwhile the great war goes thundering on. I hope you are cheery about it, and have faith in something and somebody. The slave power must be utterly annihilated. There can be no peace without that done, and for that I devoutly pray." Longfellow's statement of hostility toward the South is just one of many that were expressed by the twisted minds coming from the members of the Radical Club of Boston. These so-called intellectual elites would meet together on a regular basis for the sole purpose of the discussion of issues of national concern so that they could more effectively influence cultural and political change.

Among the many members and supporters of The Radical Club philosophies was the well-known Unitarian Transcendentalist James Freeman Clarke. He pastored the famous "Church of the Disciples" in Boston and was a close friend of Julia Ward Howe and her husband, Dr. Samuel Gridley Howe. Dr. Howe was a champion and financial benefactor of several social projects and the abolitionist activities of John Brown. Pastor Clarke, with many other of his religious fellow travelers, stressed the humanity of Jesus while minimizing and often denying His Divinity. They taught such heresies as the innate goodness of all men while denying the Biblical doctrine of the total depravity of man. This same crowd readily accepted the unproven evolutionary theories of Charles Darwin which he advocated in his book *The Origin of Species*.

The personal moral character and beliefs of many of the social reformers of the pre-war North were a direct reflection of the liberal Biblical interpretations of their religious leaders. In fact, the best known religious leader who was popular and in demand for his socio-religious and oratorical sermons was Henry Ward Beecher. He himself set no moral standard to follow in his personal life and was responsible for inflaming the citizens of the North against the South with his sermons known as 'Beecher's Bullets.' Beecher, who was born in 1813, at an early age soon became an avid follower of the social reform movement. He soon became a very liberal Congregational minister who openly advocated abolitionism and women's suffrage. He also readily adopted evolutionary theories and scientific Biblical criticism. The *New Encyclopedia Britannica* (Vol. 2, p. 43) offers this view on his personal life. "Beecher, always considered an emotional and sensual man, became in the 1870's the subject of rumours alleging immoral affairs, and he was sued in 1874 by his former friend and literary protegé Theodore Tilton, who charged him with adultery with his wife. Two ecclesiastical tribunals exonerated Beecher, though the jury in the civil suit failed to reach agreement, as have later students of the evidence. Despite the scandal, however, he remained active and influential until his death." **This is a clear example of when a society loses its moral values, even the vile and depraved continue to hold a place of high esteem in the public eye.**

The true political and philosophical colors of many of the anti-South crowd were clearly seen after the war when the social and cultural reformers were gloating in their supposed victory over the dead body of the conservative South. For example, Elizabeth Cady Stanton who was born in New York in 1815 was one of the first women to study law and to utilize her profession to further her ideals of social reform. In 1840, she married a staunch abolitionist, Henry Stanton, and they both became firm believers in the principle of the separation of church and state. She took the liberty to revise the Bible and therefore created her own called *"The Woman's Bible."*

She believed that traditional religion suppressed women, so therefore, in her arrogance she set about to liberate her gender from the restraints of Biblical authority. In 1869, she founded the National Women Suffrage Association to liberate women from the restraints and standards of male authority and to proclaim self-sovereignty. She and her cohorts advocated the right of divorce and abortion as part of the women's rights agenda.

In 1895 at the age of 80 years old, she formed an International Committee consisting of liberal preachers, social activists, free-thinkers and Bible critics as a last effort to liberalize every aspect of American culture.

Another feminist, social reformer and women suffrage leader, Belva Ann B. Lockwood, was born in 1830 at Royalton, New York. She first became a schoolteacher and then a lawyer in 1873. She feverishly worked for women's rights, equal pay for women government employees and for women lawyers to practice before the Supreme Court. She, therefore, was the first woman in the United States to practice before that high court. In 1884 and 1888, she was nominated as the United States Presidential candidate for the National Equal Rights Party to run for the highest political office in the country.

During the last half of the nineteenth century in the North, it became very evident as to what the long-range plans of the abolitionists really were. They were not a holy band of noble warriors fighting to alleviate the injustices of Negro slavery. Instead, they only used the issue of Negro slavery in the South as a public facade to hide their true agenda. The Northern pre-war abolitionists were bona-fide social revolutionaries whose purpose it was to completely overthrow the national consensus of Christian laws, morals and values upon which America was established and to a large degree still depended. Thus, they aimed their big guns of propaganda against Southern culture, because it represented everything that was despicable and was an obstacle in achieving their utopian socialist goals.

At this time, America offered such a broad arena of social reform that socialists from England and Europe were attracted to these shores to join in the fray to overthrow traditional American society. One such foreigner was Ernestine L. Rose. She was born Sismondi Potowski, a Jewess of Poland, whose father was a Rabbi. Before leaving Europe, she campaigned against social inequalities and religious or Christian tyranny. She moved to England and came under the influence of Robert Owen, the founder of English *Utopian Socialism*. She later married the abolitionist William H. Rose and moved to the United States. She soon met and aligned herself with the likes of Susan B. Anthony, Lucy Stone, Wendel Phillips, Julia Ward Howe, William L. Garrison and Elizabeth Cady Stanton. She was readily accepted and added passion, intellect and audacity to the U. S. social reform movement.

Personal moral values were openly challenged during this time and thereby precipitated a public and private moral decline that has continued to this day. With the blessings of the self-appointed social reformers, a young Jewess from New Orleans began to make bold moves in public. Adah Isaacs Menken was one of the first to bob her hair and dared to bare her body on public stage and become the forerunner of the modern strip tease act.

The above examples help to describe the social climate that was formulating in the pre-war North and thus became a major influence upon Northern psyche in shaping their opinions about Southern culture. In the pre-war South, society at large was still governed by a strong Protestant, Biblical form of social values. These two diverse cultures would eventually clash in a head-on collision which resulted in a devastating military conflict. Its affects are still being felt in the present day American religious, social and political structure.

One clear example of pure hatred that poured from the lips of Northern political leaders helps us understand the attitude of the average Union soldier. As they raped, ravaged and plundered the South, no doubt they felt justified in their actions because they were responding against the very institutions they had been taught to hate. The venomous words of Pennsylvania Representative Thaddeus Stevens sums up the attitude of anti-Southern hostility. His idea of harsh Yankee rule over the South was to "hang the leaders - crush the South - arm the Negroes - confiscate the land . . . Our generals have a sword in one hand and shackles in the other . . . The South must be punished under the rules of war, its land confiscated . . . These offending states were out of the Union and in the role of a belligerent nation to be dealt with by the laws of war and conquest."

There was not only physical abuse and desecration of church buildings in the South by Federal troops fueled by social and political hostility, but also a more subtle abuse by Northern churchmen. In many instances, Northern leaders of religious denominations would take unfair advantage over their weakened Southern denominational churches. This they did in order to silence Southern clergy in their spiritual and philosophical defense and support of the Confederate cause. The McKendree Chapel Affair was a prime example of ecclesiastical control. Methodist Bishop Matthew Simpson advocated appointing Northern or Union Loyalist ministers to the empty pulpits of Southern churches. By 1863, the war had taken a severe toll upon many churches. Many Methodist Episcopal Church, South ministers had joined the Confederate forces or were forced to flee ahead of the Federal troops in order to avoid being forced to take the 'Oath of Allegiance.'

Bishop Simpson advocated Northern church 'missionaries' to take possession of Southern churches. Michael J. Cramer, the brother in law to General U. S. Grant, used his influence to take control of the McKendree Chapel in Nashville, TN. After Southern pastors petitioned Lincoln and Andrew Johnson, the military governor of Tennessee and received a favorable verdict, Pastor Cramer refused to leave. The Northern church leadership was adamant in their position because they considered the South to be teaching a spurious Christianity.

Treatment of Southern clergy by Federal occupational forces ranged from lenient to extremely severe. Regardless of the severity of the treatment, the fact remains that the Northern political and military forces usurped their unlawful authority outside of their jurisdiction in a geographical area in which they did not belong. The following account, given by W. Harrison Daniel, is an overall view of the treatment that transpired throughout the South.

"It seems that the ministers who were forced to take the oath of loyalty to the United States government or who were removed from their churches were those whose attitude was sullen or hostile, or they were men who persisted in "political preaching" and were uncooperative with the Federal commanders. William H. Mitchell, pastor of the Presbyterian Church in Florence, Alabama, prayed for the success of Confederate arms when some Federal soldiers were attending worship, and he was arrested and imprisoned for six months. When Andrew Johnson was the military governor of Tennessee, he arrested and imprisoned for a short time three Nashville ministers because they prayed for the success of Confederate arms and refused to pray for the government of the United States. When New Orleans was occupied by Federal forces three Episcopal clergymen were arrested and deported to New York City because they refused to pray for the President of the United States; a Presbyterian minister in New Orleans was refused permission to occupy his pulpit and was ordered to leave the city.

"When Knoxville, Tennessee, was occupied by Northern troops in the fall of 1863, a number of Confederate sympathizers were deported to the cotton states, and among them were three ministers. A few ministers in East Tennessee were arrested and sent to the North as prisoners of war; and in Liberty and Marietta, Georgia, Leesburg, Alexandria, Norfolk, and Portsmouth, Virginia clergymen were arrested and imprisoned by Federal authorities. Usually this action was prompted by the clergyman's continued prayers for Confederate forces or by his refusal to pray for President Lincoln.

"There is evidence of Federal intimidation of some clergymen in many areas of the South; however, "most of the clergymen who fell before the might of Federal authorities were released soon after their arrest and were permitted to continue preaching." Perhaps the case of William F. Broaddus might illustrate the treatment of a Confederate clergyman by Federal authorities. Broaddus, who was pastor of the Baptist church in Fredericksburg, Virginia, was arrested by Federal agents at his home on July 29, 1862 and sent to Washington, where he was imprisoned for two months. During this time he was permitted to have visitors, to read his Bible and newspapers, and to receive mail. He was treated courteously by the officers, and on August 29, was paroled and sent to Richmond as an emissary to secure the release of several imprisoned Union men. The mission was a success, and by the end of September, Broaddus had been released and was back in Fredericksburg performing his ministerial duties.

"Undoubtedly Federal authorities would have been pleased to have captured such zealous and "fire-eating" clergymen as Benjamin M. Palmer, James H. Thornwell, and Stephen Elliott. But the most passionate members of the clergy escaped Federal agents and were never caught. Those clergymen who were subject to indignities were the quieter, less zealous men, who did not flee from the enemy but remained to care for their parishioners and to suffer with them. It appears that those Southern clergymen who were arrested and imprisoned were exceptions to the treatment accorded most ministers. The vast majority of Southern clergymen were not molested and were permitted to continue their ministerial duties. Nevertheless, the uncertainties which the Church encountered with military authorities and the intimidation which was either actual or potential impeded denominational programs and helped to disrupt the function of the Church. As a result of the war all of the denominations faced a major rebuilding task in the spring of 1865."

From *Southern Protestantism in the Confederacy* by W. Harrison Daniel, pp. 163-165.

In sharp contrast to the religious liberalism of the North was the strong evangelical form of Protestant Christianity throughout the South. The majority of Southern Christians were adherents to the Calvinistic persuasion of Protestantism with the exception of many of the Methodists and other smaller groups. During this time, many of the Southern clergy viewed the creation of the Confederacy as the working of the sovereign hand of Almighty God. They often compared it to the establishment of the Old Testament Kingdom of Israel under David and considered the people as a 'chosen people' in fulfilling their God ordained destiny as a nation.

Without prejudice, it is obvious to see that the social and religious structure of Northern society was by and large influenced by prosperity, humanism, and materialism which in turn resulted in greed, moral corruption and spiritual decadence. Many of the South's philosophers and theologians viewed secession not only as a political separation from an unconstitutional Federal government, but also as a religious separation in order to maintain religious and social purity. They placed a major emphasis upon the preservation of their ancestral and religious heritage. The War For Southern Independence was not only a political and military conflict, but it was also the climax of an on-going holy war.

Throughout the history of the War, there are scores of accounts where both clergy, civil and military leaders admonished the Southern people to pray, repent and place total dependence upon the Lord of Hosts in their struggle against the forces of evil. From an army camp Presbyterian minister, Charles C. Jones, Jr. wrote, "The nation must be brought to feel their sins and their dependence upon God, not only for their blessings but for their actual salvation from the many and huge dangers which surround us." The call for national repentance also came in the form of a proclamation by President Jefferson Davis for days of fasting and humiliation. There were nine days of national fasting called between June 1861 and March 1865, plus many more proclaimed by state governors and legislatures.

A high water mark of Southern culture was its climate which helped produce some highly distinguished scholars and theologians. These were men of high learning, keen intellect and perception and a deep passion for the purity of the Gospel of Jesus Christ. Possessing a Christian world view of human history and civilization, they therefore measured all the actions and institutions of men according to the righteous standards of God's Word. Among the many worthies of that time were such men as Presbyterian clergymen Robert L. Dabney, James H. Thornwell and Benjamin M. Palmer who were stalwarts in their defense for conservative Biblical interpretation. They stood in stark contrast to the advocates of Biblical higher-criticism that were prevalent in many Northern seminaries such as Princeton and Harvard. Without doubt, God had raised up these men as a conscience for the whole of American society, both North and South. In his perception and analysis of the two cultures in conflict, James Henley Thornwell, theologian and professor at Columbia Theological Seminary (SC) made the following insightful observation.

"The parties to this conflict are not merely abolitionists and slaveholders – They are atheists, socialists, communists, red republicans, Jacobins, on the one side, and the friends of order and regulated freedom on the other. In one word, the world is a battleground – Christianity and atheism are the combatants and the progress of humanity is at stake".

After suffering such a devastating military defeat, enduring such desecration of church property and a rude denominational takeover, Southern clergy and churches began to change their post-war view of the role of religion in secular society. Where they once stressed the Biblical authority of Jesus Christ and Mosaic Law in the governing of society, they began to emphasize strictly the personal aspect of religion. To their merit, conservative Southern churchmen rejected the "Social Gospel" of the Northern social reform movements in favor of a more "fundamental" and evangelical approach to Biblical interpretation. On the other hand, through spiritual gradualism, churchmen in both the North and the South began to accept an eschatology of defeat and spiritual escapism. This came about largely through the introduction of the prophetic viewpoint known as "futurism." The introduction of this anti-Biblical doctrine of John Nelson Darby of England's Plymouth Brethren movement, into the American religious scene has had devastating affects upon the church's influence in secular society. This has helped bring about the ever encroaching and misunderstood philosophy of the "separation of church and state."

The attack against Biblical Christianity has moved from a physical desecration of church property and the arrest of ministers to an even more subtle form of harassment and control. This present day method is by far more effective in achieving its desired end. This method is a combination of such sinister forces as syncretism or the blending of incongruous belief systems such as paganism, multiculturalism and equalitarianism with Biblical Christianity. Therefore, the whole of American society is now experiencing a cultural, racial and religious apostasy. **Militarily, the South lost the war on the battlefield, but it was western civilization as a whole that lost in its churches, schools, state houses, homes, and in the minds and souls of its people.**

Without doubt, the physical and moral devastation that was brought about in the South because of the unscrupulous actions of both the Northern radical politicians and its military power is unequaled in American history. Their ultimate intentions were to forever change the cultural, social, spiritual and racial values of the Southern people and their institutions. The physical desecration of Southern houses of worship by the military forces and the attempted ecclesiastical takeover of church leadership by Northern denominational officials is proof that the Southern churches and clergy had to be removed or conquered. This had to be accomplished before their intended cultural cleansing could be completed. Southern culture had to be decapitated, because Biblical Protestant Christianity was its head.

While the Southern congregations back home were suffering physical and moral defeats, thousands of 'soldiers in gray' were experiencing revival in the trenches. Throughout the Confederate Armies, the spirit of revival was being felt by privates and officers alike. Through the anointed ministry of God's Word by faithful chaplains, ministers and colporteurs, the spiritual atmosphere of a vast portion of the army was being changed from indifference to concern and genuine repentance. Many denominational chaplains serving in the army laid aside their doctrinal differences and supported this most unusual and sovereign move of God.

During this revival, religious services among the soldiers were held not only in crudely constructed chapels, but in the camps, open fields, the woods, the trenches and even on the field of battle itself. Sometimes prayer meetings were held throughout the day and often lasted until sunrise. Not only privates, but many high ranking officers were the recipients of the saving grace of Jesus Christ as real spiritual conviction of sin would grip the hearts of war-hardened soldiers. The revival which took place within the ranks of the Confederate forces during the War for Southern Independence was nothing short of a supernatural work of spiritual renewal and cultural preservation. It was the true religious high-water mark in America that would preserve and guide true Biblical Christianity in both the North and the South for succeeding generations. It was a major divine event that would determine a regional cultural Christian consensus and consequently designate the South as the *"Bible Belt"* of the nation.

We, the descendants of those noble Southerners who earnestly believed and fought for what they knew was right, need to arise out of our sleep and once again defend our Southern heritage. An old song of the Huguenots should be our prayer today; "Spirit who made them live, Awaken their children, so that they will know how to follow them." Many well-meaning modern day patriots are following the slogan of the old Southern Democrats. That is to be faithful "to the Constitution as it is and to the Union as it was." Western civilization's only hope of restoration and reformation lies not in the Constitution, the Union or any other of the lofty yet faulty deeds of men. Our only hope is in the appearance of our coming Redeemer, the Lord Jesus Christ and His coronation as the King of Kings and Lord of Lords (Revelation 19:11-16).

EXAMPLES OF NORTHERN PROPAGANDA

In the propaganda warfare against the South, the writers and poets of the religio-social self-appointed liberal elite took every opportunity to blame the South for the national tragedy of war. In 1861, Henry Wadsworth Longfellow wrote a poem during a time of personal depression, after the tragic death of his second wife and while worrying about his son in the Union Army. In this poem, he again expressed his feelings of blame toward the South. This poem was later set to music and became a popular Christmas carol, I Heard The Bells on Christmas Day. Some of the original verses which are quoted below are generally omitted from modern hymn books.

I HEARD THE BELLS ON CHRISTMAS DAY

I heard the bells on Christmas Day
Their old familiar carols play,
Then from each black, accursed mouth
The cannon thundered in the South,
And with the sound, the carols drowned
Of peace on earth, good-will to men!

It was as if an earthquake rent
The hearth-stones of a continent,
And made forlorn
The households born
Of peace on earth, good-will to men!

And in despair I bowed my head;
"There is no peace on earth," I said:
"For hate is strong,
And mocks the song
Of peace on earth, good-will to men!"

Then pealed the bells more loud and deep:
"God is not dead; nor doth he sleep!
The Wrong shall fail,
The Right prevail,
With peace on earth, good-will to men

BATTLE HYMN OF THE REPUBLIC

There are many beautiful, inspiring, spiritual hymns and songs of the Christian church that were born out of adversity, during times of revival or God's rich dealings with His servants. These songs and hymns we must deeply revere and appreciate for their rich meaning and spiritual value.

However, there are some songs that have been adopted into Christian hymnody that do not belong there because of their history, and/or doctrine. One such song that has crept into the Christian church and its worship, unnoticed, is the song entitled, "The Battle Hymn of the Republic". This song should not be considered a hymn of our Faith, because of its sinister origin, the attitude and actions that it promoted, and the liberal philosophy of its authoress, Mrs. Julia Ward Howe.

First, concerning Mrs. Howe, she is commonly known as a writer and social reformer, and not as a Bible-believing Christian. After her marriage to Dr. Samuel Gridley Howe in 1843, they moved to Boston and became associated with the famous Unitarian "Church of the Disciples", pastored by the well-known Unitarian transcendentalist, James Freeman Clarke.

Mrs. Howe and her husband became deeply involved in the anti-slavery movement of the 1840's and 50's and edited one of its papers, the "Boston Commonwealth". In her zeal
and desire for social reform at any cost, Mrs. Howe came to revere the basest of men such as John Brown, the Kansas murderer and terrorist.

After the infamous murdering rampage at Harper's Ferry when John Brown was condemned to die, **Mrs. Howe believed that "John Brown's death will be holy and glorious. John Brown will glorify the gallows like Jesus glorified the cross."**

As a Unitarian, her religious views were not based on the fundamental theocentric (God-centered) doctrines of the Scriptures, but upon the 19th century liberal anthropocentric (man-centered) beliefs of the higher critics, poetic mystics and the advocates of transcendental meditation. These beliefs can be briefly summed up as the fatherhood of God and the brotherhood of all men.

By her own statements it is very clear as to what her opinion was concerning Jesus Christ. She said, "Not until the Civil War did I officially join the Unitarian Church and accept the fact that Christ was merely a great teacher with no higher claim to preeminence in wisdom, goodness and power than many other men.

"Having rejected the exclusive doctrine that made Christianity and special forms of it the only way of spiritual redemption, **I now accept the belief that not only Christians but all human beings, no matter what their religion, are capable of redemption**." These are the same fallacies and heresies which are espoused by the religious and academic liberal establishment yet today. On the occasion of the writing of the words of the song "The Battle Hymn of the Republic", with the blessings of President Lincoln, she wrote words to a popular tune of the day that could be used as a rallying cry of the North in support of their invasion of the Christian South.

The message of this song, shrouded in religious terms was intended to convince the people of the North that they were involved in a "holy war" for a righteous cause.

Simply stated, it was used as typical war propaganda by the Lincoln administration for brainwashing the citizens of the North in their bloody invasion and destruction of the South.

Ever since Mrs. Howe wrote the words to this song in December 1861, many sincere well-meaning Christians have unknowingly sung this song with religious zeal and fervor without understanding its original intent and meaning. Along with other prominent Unitarians, as Mrs. Howe viewed the Union troops of the "Army of the Potomac", she was then inspired to write the words that are known and sung today.

She portrayed the Union Army as the "glory of the coming of the Lord" going to "trample out the vintage where the grapes of wrath are stored". She plainly states that "I have seen Him (God) in the watchfires of a hundred circling (Union) camps." To her, Lincoln's 75,000 volunteers were the "Army of God" going forth to slaughter the evil resisters of social reform and progressive centralized government.

The "burnished rows of steel" that she mentioned referred to the polished Union cannons that rained down death and destruction upon not only the Confederate soldier, but also upon southern cities and countryside.

At this time in American history, "The South" was quite different in many ways from the North. The South was more agrarian while the North was more industrialized. The South more rural while the North more urban; the South advocated the traditional interpretation of the Constitutional principles of our American Founding Fathers for States Rights, and local governmental control as opposed to the Northern Republican party view of centralized governmental powers; the people of the South were more traditional in maintaining their culture dating back to their Celtic ancestors, whereas the North was rapidly losing the racial and cultural traditions through the influx of more liberal ideas of equalitarianism; the educational institutions of the South were more conservative in thought and practice as opposed to the Northern concepts of universalism, humanism, deism and rationalism that had crept into its once great academic institutions such as Harvard and Yale; at this critical time in our history the South was definitely more adamant in its stalwart defense of traditional Calvinistic Christianity that dated back to the early reformers while the religious establishments of the North were accepting and promoting the fallacious anti-Biblical concepts of the more modernistic approach to such truths as the authenticity and inerrancy of the Scriptures.

Bibliography

History of St. James Parish, 1729-1979, by Leora Hiatt McEachern, 1982

Southern Historical Society Papers, Vol. 29, 1901

A Fairfield Sketchbook by Julian S. Bolick located in the Camden, South Carolina Archives

A History of Washington County, Georgia 1784-1989 published by The Washington County Historical Society

Christ in the Camp, J. William Jones, Confederate Chaplain

Deeds of Daring by Both Blue and Gray by D. M. Kelsey, J. L. Hebert Publishing Co. 1887, pp. 139, 142, 143

Embattled Confederates by Bell Irvin Wiley (pp. 194-195)

Fighting For Time of The Image of War 1861-1865 Vol. 4, National Historical Society 1983, p. 116

Fighting For Time Vol. 4 of The Image of War 1861-1865, the National Historical Society

I Heard The Bells on Christmas Day, Henry Wadsworth Longfellow, 1861

Indian Creek Baptist Church - paper written at the request of DeKalb County, GA Historical Society by Elizabeth Austin Ford, 1950

Jasper County - The Gateway to South Carolina and The

Lowcountry Jasper County Chamber of Commerce, Ridgeland, South Carolina

Lancaster News article by Leland Summers dated November 10, 2000, Ex-Confederates Show Compassion For Foes

Letter, which is a republication from the Alderson, West Virginia, *Statesman*, October 29, 1883

Merchant of Terror or General Sherman and Total War by John B. Walters 1973

Narrative of the Great Revival which Prevailed in the Southern Armies, William Bennett, D.D., Confederate Chaplain

New Encyclopedia Britannica (Vol. 2, p. 43)

Ninety Years in Aiken County, South Carolina by Gasper L. Toole, II

Our Incredible Civil War (1960) by Burke Davis

Photographic History of the Civil War Vol. 2, Francis T. Miller, Editor in Chief

Preachers with Power by Douglas F. Kelly, *The Banner of Truth Trust*, 1992 p. 167

Shadow of a Mighty Rock, A Social and Cultural History of Presbyterianism in Marshall County, Mississippi by Robert Milton Winter, pp. 179-182, 191 & 192

Sheridan - The Life and Wars of Gen. Phil Sheridan (pp. 178-179) by Ray Morris, Jr.

Sherman's March by Burke Davis

Southern Historical Society Papers Vol. 29, 1901, letter published March, 1884

Southern Protestantism in the Confederacy by W. Harrison Daniel, 1989

The Embattled Confederacy Vol. 3 of The Image of War 1861-1865, National Historical Society 1982

The First Twenty Years of the History of St. Paul's Evangelical Lutheran Church, G. D. Bernheim, D.D., 1879

The Lost Cause (1886) by E. A. Pollard

The Lost Cause by E. A. Pollard as reported by the Daily Phoenix

The Origin of Species, Charles Darwin

The Photographic History of the Civil War - The Armies and Leaders, Poetry and Eloquence, Vol. 5

The Shenandoah Valley of Virginia 1861-1865 A War Story by Sanford C. Kellogg 1903

The Siege of Savannah in December 1864 and The Operations in Georgia and The Third Military District of South Carolina During General Sherman's March From Atlanta to the Sea by Charles C. Jones, Jr. 1874

The South Besieged Vol. 5 of The Image of War 1861-1865, the National Historical Society, 1983

The Wilmington Campaign - Last Days of Departing Hope by Chris E. Fonvielle, Jr.

The Woman's Bible, Elizabeth Cady Stanton

True Tales of the South at War collected and edited by Clarence Poe

Welcome to Lancaster South Carolina 1785 - A Walking Tour For Visitors Guide

William Wallace's Civil War Letters: The Virginia Campaign, edited by John O. Holzhueter, stored in the Milwaukee Historical Society, an entry by William Wallace of Banks Division, Wisconsin Regiment

THE TWIN MERCHANTS OF DESTRUCTION AND GREED

NORTHERN ABOLITIONISTS
AND
CARPETBAGGERS

NORTHERN ABOLITIONISTS

*WHAT DID THE NORTHERN ABOLITIONISTS
REALLY BELIEVE AND SAY?*

CONTRARY TO POPULAR BELIEF THEIR GOAL WAS NOT "FREEDOM FOR ALL MEN" BUT THE DESTRUCTION OF SOUTHERN CULTURE AND CONSTITUTIONAL GOVERNMENT

Of all the social and political movements to transpire upon the American continent, the destructive forces of nineteenth century Northern abolitionism has been the most devastating and lasting in its results in undermining the moral, social, political and spiritual fabric of our nation. Posing as a religious and humanitarian cause in order to abolish the institution of slavery, the zealots of abolitionism were willing to bring about the downfall of the American Republic for which they feignly fought to save.

The forces of abolitionism were so furious that men and women at every level of Northern society were overwhelmed by its deviant and deceitful philosophy.

They believed that any 'means justified the end'. This included not only the intelligentsia of the movement such as the politicians in Congress, 'Christian' ministers preaching their fiery perverted 'gospel', businessmen committed to financing the cause, but insurrectionists committing brutal acts of murder and criminal terrorism.

Regardless of the severe price that the nation, both North and South, would have to pay in order to accomplish their goal, they believed that war would eventually bring about their desired utopia. Thus the liberal media convinced the majority of the Northern populace to support Lincoln's war of aggression upon the South to eradicate the evils of slavery. To this day the **liberal media manufactured issue of slavery** is set forth as the primary cause of the so-called 'Civil War'.

Ten years before the war, the prominent Presbyterian pastor and theology professor, James H. Thornwell of Columbia Theological Seminary in South Carolina, said:

"The parties to this conflict are not merely abolitionists and slaveholders - they are atheists, socialists, communists, red Republicans, Jacobins, on the one side, and the friends of order and regulated freedom on the other. In one word, the world is a battleground - Christianity and atheism are the combatants and the progress of humanity is at stake."

Following are statements by several nineteenth century abolitionists and their fellow-travelers:

Pastor Henry Clay Fish, First Baptist Church of Newark , NJ, November 1863; "...The war successfully ended...**treason and traitors expelled from the country; the heresy of state sovereignty and secession killed;..."**

Henry Wadsworth Longfellow "Meanwhile the great war goes thundering on. I hope you are cheery about it, and have faith in something and somebody. The slave power must be utterly annihilated. There can be no peace without that done; and for that I devoutly pray."

Ralph Waldo Emerson
Concerning The War for Southern Independence he said: "If it costs ten years and ten to recover the general prosperity, the destruction of the South is worth so much." In 1859 before John Brown was executed, Emerson referred to Brown as "The Saint, whose fate yet hangs in suspense, but whose martyrdom, if it shall be perfected, will make the gallows as glorious as the Cross."

Wendell Phillips
Lawyer, became president of Anti-slavery Society in 1865, advocate of the 13th, 14th and 15th amendments to the Constitution, social activist said: "The Constitution of our fathers was a mistake. Tear it to pieces and make a better. Don't say the machine is out of order; it is in

order; it does what the framers intended-protect slavery.
Our aim is disunion, breaking up the states! I have shown
you that our work cannot be done under our
institutions...No man has a right to be surprised at this state
of things. It is just what we abolitionists and disunionists
have attempted to bring about. It is the first sectional party
ever organized in this country. It does not know its own
face, and calls itself national; but it is not national - it is
sectional. ***The Republican party is a party of the North***
pledged against the South."

"The land is ours-confiscated, guaranteed; its title
given to the soldier who has finished his service. Give it to
the black man, who is willing to take it, and plant a state,
under the guarantee of the Union-employ free labor upon
that fertile soil, and commence again the civil machinery,
the organization of a state... "I know that it seems
something like absolute barbarian conquest, I allow it. ***I***
don't believe there will be any peace until 347,000 slaves
holders are either hung or exiled. History shows no
precedent of getting rid of an aristocracy like this, except by the
death of the generation."

William Lloyd Garrison Journalist,
president of Anti-slavery Society
from 1843-1865 - abolitionist fanatic
said: "This Union is a lie! The
American Union is an imposition -- a
covenant with death, and an
agreement with hell!...I am for its
overthrow!...Up with the flag of
disunion, that we may have a free
and glorious Republic of our own;
and when the hour shall come, the
hour will have arrived that shall
witness the overthrow of slavery."

Resolutions of the American Anti-Slavery Society:

Resolved, that secession from the United States government is the duty of every Abolitionists, since no one can take office, or deposit his vote under its constitution without violating his anti-slavery principles, and rendering himself an abettor to the slaveholder in his sin.

Resolved, That years of warfare against the slave power have convinced us that every act done in support of the American Union rivets the chain of the slave - that the only exodus of the slave to freedom, unless it be one of blood, must be over the remains of the present American Church, and the grave of the present Union.

Resolved, That the abolitionists of this country should make it one of the primary objects of this agitation, to dissolve the American Union."

Rep. Thaddeus Stevens:
"The Union as it was, and the Constitution as it is - God forbid it! We must conquer the Southern States, and hold them as conquered provinces."

Resolutions passed at a proto-Republican Convention, Boston, MA: "Resolved, That we seek a dissolution of the Union; and *Resolved,* That we do hereby declare ourselves the enemies of the Constitution, of the Union, and of the Government of the United States; and *Resolved,* That we proclaim it as our unalterable purpose and determination to live and labor for the dissolution of the present Union."

Kansas Senator James Lane:

"I would like to live long enough to see every white man in South Carolina, in hell, and the Negroes inheriting their territory. It would not wound my feelings any day to find the dead bodies of rebel sympathizers pieced with bullet holes in every street and alley of Washington. Yes, I would regret this, for I would not like to witness all this waste of powder and lead. I would rather have them hung, and the ropes saved! Let them dangle until their stinking bodies rot and fall to the ground piece by piece."

CARPETBAGGERS

"The Man with the (Carpet) Bags"

*An 1872 cartoon by Thomas Nast, depicting
the Southern attitude toward Northerners
during Reconstruction.*

**They came South with their money,
arrogance and greed to further ravage and plunder
a conquered nation!**

Unequaled in the history of modern warfare was the unjust and tyrannical treatment of the Northern Radical Republicans toward the conquered and impoverished social structure, economy and governments of the defeated Southern states following The War for Southern Independence.

A Carpetbagger, supported by bayonets, bends the back of the impoverished South

In the minds of the Northern Radicals it was not enough to militarily defeat the Southern armies on the battlefield. In order to satisfy a burning hatred toward 'all things

Southern', they determined to utterly crush the entire Southern nation. On March 2, 1867, **Congress passed the Reconstruction Act** and thereby abolished local civil government in the Southern states. It divided the South into five military districts and Federal troops were sent in as occupational forces to insure that the Southern whites were held in total subjugation to every radical Republican policy of the Northern politicians. This postwar 'Reconstruction' era lasted from 1867 to 1877.

During this *'Reconstruction'* period many Northerners, including those from the secret society of the Union League of New York and Philadelphia, came South to take unfair advantage of a ruined economic and governmental structure in order to gain political and/or financial advantage. It was charged by both white Southerners and even some Northerners that these greedy opportunists were self-seeking in their endeavor with total disregard toward the Southern people and their hardships as a result of the war. They moved South carrying all their belongings in satchels made of cheap carpeting. Thus, these unwelcome strangers became known as *Carpetbaggers.* These social agitators included lawmakers, money lenders, financial speculators, educators and even ministers. This epithet was originally and still remains a term of contempt against anyone whose purpose it is to exploit or dominate other people against their will.

Although many carpetbaggers expressed a 'concern' for the social welfare and education of the newly freed black citizens, most of them, by far, supported the corrupt schemes of the Reconstruction governments. They did this by instilling in the black population feelings of resentment, revenge and even violence against their former white masters and enlisted them into secret clubs. Under the guise of 'educating' the newly made citizens of the black population, they placed in them a false hope of political power and financial success. The Negro's attempt to fulfill this dream as a free man generally resulted in deep disappointment and failure due to the carpetbaggers false and utopian promises and the Negroes' idealistic expectations. The Southern Negroes thinking that they were now free, became nothing more than expendable pawns in the hands of their new 'masters', the shrewd and self-seeking Northern carpetbaggers.

A Carpetbag Legislature

"The reek of vile cigars and stale whiskey . . . was overwhelming . . . The space behind the seats of the members was strewn with corks, broken glass, stale crusts, greasy pieces of paper, and picked bones . . . Each member had his name painted in enormous gold letters on his desk, and had placed beside it a sixty-dollar French spittoon . . . The uproar was deafening. From four to six Negroes were trying to speak at the same time . . . The most of them were munching peanuts, and the crush of hulls under heavy feet added a sub note to the confusion . . . the speaker was drowned in a storm of contending yells."

—Thomas Dixon, 1904

In 1867, the leadership of state governments fell into the hands of Republican carpetbaggers and sympathetic native white Southern 'scalawags'. In writing the new state laws and constitutions, carpetbaggers included certain provisions to strengthen Federal power and the liberated Southern Negro in order to further subjugate the white population. Most of the carpetbagger governors and politicians of the ex-Confederate States were described by Horace Greeley, the editor of the New York Tribune, as men *"bent on stealing and plundering, many of them with both arms around Negroes, and their hands in their pockets, seeing if they cannot pick a paltry dollar out of them."*

There were basically three conditions that guaranteed the dictatorial rule of the Federal Government in the South during the era of 'Reconstruction'. They were: 1) strong radical Republican control of the Federal government, 2) amendments granting the Negro freedom, citizenship and the right to vote, and 3) the presence of Federal troops as occupational forces.

Many Northern Republican leaders such as Pennsylvania Representative Thaddeus Stevens expressed feelings of utter contempt for the already defeated and impoverished people of the South. His idea of harsh Yankee rule over the South was to *"hang the leaders – crush the South – arm the Negroes – confiscate the land. . . Our generals have a sword in one hand and shackles in the other . . . The South must be punished under the rules of war, its land confiscated . . . these offending states were out of the Union and in the role of a belligerent nation to be dealt with by the laws of war and conquest."* This type of harsh attitude encouraged dishonest and unscrupulous Northern carpetbaggers to engage in any ruthless scheme possible to defraud Southerners of their last remaining possessions. Many Southerners were forced to sell their farms, plantations, crops and businesses, through intimidation, to greedy Northern speculators at extreme financial losses. Carpetbagger state legislators levied heavy taxes upon the Southern people to help pay for both Union veteran pensions and war debts. These same state legislatures offered no financial assistance to the Confederate veteran, while at the same time passing laws 'legalizing' their misappropriation of public funds for their own selfish gain.

From this tragic time in American history until now, the Federal government has steadily increased its tyrannical control over all local governments and nullified the Constitutional principle of *States Rights*.

THERE WAS JOY IN THE CAMP

A Brief History of the Spiritual Revival in the Confederate Army

One of America's least known spiritual revivals saved the cultural and spiritual heritage of the nation and preserved Biblical Christianity for succeeding generations!!

There Was
JOY In The Camp

Distributing Tracts in the trenches

"It matters not what day in the week it may be, or what hour of the day, you have only to pass the word around that there will be preaching at such a point, and there will promptly assemble a large crowd of eager listeners.

No appointment for weeks, or days, or hours ahead is necessary. No church-bell summons, to gorgeous houses of worship, elegant ladies or fashionably attired men. But a few taps of the drum, a few strains of the bugle, or, better still, the singing of some old familiar hymn, serves as a 'church call' well understood, and from every part of the camp weather-beaten soldiers, in faded and tattered uniforms, hasten to the selected spot and gather close around the preacher, who, with, 'nature's great temple' for his church, and the blue canopy of heaven for his 'sounding board,' is fortunate if he have so much as a barrel or well-rounded stump for a pulpit."

The above is a brief description given by Dr. J. William Jones of the many scenes of worship that took place in the camps of the Confederate army during the great spiritual revival during the 'War for Southern Independence.'

Of all the many ways in which the Lord has blessed and enriched His people over the many centuries since He called our Father Abraham out of Ur of the Chaldees, it has been through the means of spiritual revivals. In fact, this characteristic alone is sufficient evidence to any honest heart and mind eager to accept the truth of God's promises coupled with His attribute of faithfulness to keep those promises to witness to the true identity of God's people Israel. Early in the life and call of Abraham when the Lord appeared unto him in the plains of Mamre, it is interesting to note that the Lord made a statement to the two accompanying angels that *"I know him, that he will command his children and his household after him, and they shall keep the way of the Lord, to do justice and judgement; that the Lord may bring upon Abraham that which He has spoken of him."* (Genesis 18:19)

In spite of the sinfulness and disobedience of many of Abraham's children in succeeding generations as recorded in the Old Testament account of Israel's history, the fact still stands that the Lord Himself made this prophetic declaration that Abraham would command his children and household after him and they shall keep or follow in the ways of the Lord. From this prophetic promise, it is evident that even amongst the iniquitous disobedience of the nations of Israel as a whole, there would still be many of Abraham's children who would be the recipients of spiritual revival through the supernatural manifestation of "times of refreshing [that] shall come from the presence of the Lord." (Acts 3:19)

> "In all my perplexities and distresses, the Bible has never failed to give me light and strength."
>
> --General Robert E. Lee

One such time of spiritual refreshing in our history came during one of the darkest hours of our existence as a nation. In fact, the Lord saw fit to providentially send this revival to our people during the time when we were the most divided in terms of politics, education, culture, economics and religious faith. This was during the military conflict that we know as 'The War for Southern Independence' of 1861 - 1865.

At this time in our national history, the regions of the North and South were quite different from one another in many ways. For several decades preceding the war, the natural development of these two regions seemed to go in somewhat opposite directions. The South developed as an agrarian and rural society, while the North was more industrialized and urban. The southern political leaders advocated a more traditional interpretation of our national Constitution while the northern leaders followed a more liberal view. One of the most obvious differences was in the area of religious belief and social philosophy.

Some of the established churches and prominent ministers of the North seemed to be more influenced by the unscriptural philosophies of Deism, Pantheism, Unitarianism, Humanism and rationalism which was a carry-over from the recent "reign of terror" of the French Revolution. At this same time most churches and Christian ministers of the South held to the more traditional

Calvinistic view and practice of Scripture that had been passed down from the Protestant Reformation. It just seems inevitable that the people of these two regions of the same country would eventually come to a parting of the ways or at least a clash of political, cultural and religious philosophies. Instead it came to a head in the form of a military conflict which resulted in more deaths than all other American wars combined.

During this time of national crisis when seemingly our nation was the most divided, the Lord in His sovereign mercy saw fit to send a mighty spiritual revival to the Confederate Army of the South with such powerful effects that it would still be felt to this day. The spiritual impact of this great revival helped to solidify what we still call the "Bible Belt." The revival that took place would affect many of the officers and common soldiers of the three main divisions of the Southern Army, but mainly The Army of Northern Virginia of which Robert E. Lee was the commanding general. When this army was formed, little did the officers and soldiers realize that they were coming together not only to fight a war, but to experience the greatest supernatural move of Almighty God ever to take place in an active war time army.

With the official authorization and the moral support of President Jefferson Davis and General Robert E. Lee, many pastors and evangelists would hold religious services in the camps while the army was idle between campaigns, immediately before many battles and even during the heat of battle itself. One of the most prominent chaplains who was mightily used of God in leading soldiers to Christ, J. William Jones D.D., in his book entitled "Christ In The Camp," gives the following account as a typical scene when many young men left their homes and loved ones to go places unknown to fight for their country.

He writes, *"an hour before the appointed (departure) time that splendid company . . . marched to the depot where an immense crowd had assembled to see them off. An aged minister of the gospel (now gone to his reward) spoke words of earnest counsel, and led in a fervent prayer that the God of Jacob might go forth with these young men, keep them in the way whither they went, and bring them back to their homes in peace and safety - but, above all, that he would shield them from the vices of the camp and lead them into paths of righteousness."* **Truly, there was faith in the camp.**

Chaplain Jones goes on to recall the story of one young soldier who found that "the camp had not proven to him a 'school of vice', but on the contrary, he had learned there the preciousness of his mother's Bible, and had gone with simple faith to her Savior. And as the last hour drew near, he met death with calm resignation and said to the weeping loved ones who stood around: *"I trust in Jesus and am not afraid to die,"* . . .

A young captain lay in agony on the small cot in the overcrowded hospital. The chaplain, a gray-haired man of over 60 winters, stood by the captain in his dying moments . . . knelt by the soldier's bed and began to sing:

> **Just as I am, without one please,**
> **But that Thy blood was shed for me,**
> **And that Thou bidd'st me come to Thee,**
> **O Lamb of God, I come, I come.**

From Chaplain's in Gray

Another chaplain, Rev. J. C. Granberry, D.D., Bishop of the Methodist Episcopal Church South gives a brief description of the rejoicing and exhilaration experienced by soldiers on both sides of the conflict. He records, "...*godly men who followed the Stars and Stripes will thank God for the evidence that the soldiers who opposed them with constancy and valor, many shedding their lifeblood on the field, where partakers of like precious faith with themselves. To me it is a happy thought that in the two confronting camps, often at the same hour, there rose with voice and heart the common strain, "All Hail the Power of Jesus' Name!"*

The tone of the preaching by the pastors and chaplains in the Army of Northern Virginia was evangelical in nature and as recorded by Dr. Granberry, it stressed *"eternal things, the claims of God, the worth of the soul, the wages of sin which is death, and the gift of God which is eternal life through Jesus Christ our Lord - these were the matter of preaching... the songs, prayers, lay testimonies and exhortation, in a word, all the exercises, were in the same line. There was no stirring up of bad blood; no inflaming of malice and revenge. The man of God lifted up, not the Stars and Bars, but the Cross, and pressed the inquiry, 'who among you are on the Lord's side?'"*

"Reverend Tom J. Stokes in his letter to his sister presented his portrayal of the revivals in April. On April 5, 1864, he wrote that at the close of one meeting, the chaplain invited mourners to the "anxious seat." For thirty minutes, they came from every part of the great congregation, many with streaming eyes to give the old preacher their hand to ask for prayer from God's people. "Men who never shrank in battle from any responsibility came forward weeping. Such is the power of the Gospel of

Christit when preached in its purity." "Born Again in the Trenches: Revivalism in the Confederate Army" by Dr. G. Clinton Prim, Jr. pg 164

Dr.Granberry goes on to describe the general atmosphere in many camps when he said, *"certainly our soldiers were exposed to severe temptations, and deprived of many aids to pious culture. Yet grace triumphed over all these disadvantages. I have nowhere witnessed more complete, symmetrical and beautiful examples of Christian character than in the army. Some of them were boys, others mature men, some in the ranks, others officers of various grades. Away from the happy influences of neighborhood and home, they were chaste, temperate, and pure."*

"Cut off from church and Sunday school, often having no day of sacred rest and little communion of saints, they feared the Lord and thought often upon His name. On every march they carried the well-thumbed Bible, and the hard ground on which they lay without a pillow, bed or tent, often proved to them a Bethel . . . They delighted in devotional meetings, and were not ashamed to witness for Christ." **Truly there was joy in the camp**.

"Religion is the theme. Everywhere, you hear around the camp fires at night the sweet song of Zion. This spirit pervades the whole army... What a change, what a change! When one year ago card playing and profane language seemed to be the order of the day. Now, what is the cause of this change? Manifestly the working of God's Spirit" Prim pg. 165

Down through the centuries of time, the atmosphere of the army has been regarded as demoralizing to most men which has been described in the proverb 'the worse the man the better the soldier'. The same would have been true for General Lee's Army of Northern Virginia except for the overflowing presence of the God of all grace that intervened in the hearts and lives of thousands of its men.

Within the depraved heart of every man due to the sinful nature inherited from our father Adam is the tendency to commit sin, ignore responsibility toward God for our lives and to willfully live apart from righteousness and seek the ways of pleasure in this present world. Many a soldier in the ranks of the Confederate Army no doubt had it in his heart and mind that this would be his chance to enjoy the pleasures of sin while away from home. Among the vices that many of the men engaged in, drunkenness, profanity, gambling and Sabbath breaking were the most prominent. In spite of these initial chronic sins, Dr. Jones states with confidence, *"but I shall be able to show, on the other hand, that Jesus was in our camps with wonderful power, and that no army in all history - not even Cromwell's 'Roundheads' - had in it as much of real, evangelical religion and devout piety as the Army of Northern Virginia."*

Among the many touching scenes that took place during this time of spiritual revival were the water baptismal services conducted by the chaplains and visiting pastors. Dr. Jones writes that *". . . when the orders for moving came to A. P. Hill's corps near Fredericks- burg, they found chaplains J. J. Hyman and E. B. Barrett, of Georgia engaged in baptizing in Massaponax Creek some of the converts in the revival . . ."* on Sunday, June 29, 1863 near Hagerstown, Maryland, *". . . the banks of the historic Antietam were lined with an immense crowd of Confederate soldiers, but they came not in 'battle array' - no opposing host confronted them - no cannon belched its hoarse thunder - and the shriek of shell and the whistle of the minnie were unheard."*

Instead of these, sweet strains of the songs of Zion were wafted on the breeze, and the deepest solemnity pervaded the gathered host as one of the chaplains led down into the historic stream fourteen veterans who a few months before had fought at Sharpsburg, and were now enlisting under the banner of the Cross." **Truly, there was joy in the camp.**

"Dr. Burrows Preaching in his Shirt sleeves."
"Well, if you and your people can stand my filling your pulpit n this garb, I reckon I can."

"A chaplain-historian, in an evaluation of the Dalton evangelistic efforts, wrote: The work at Dalton while the army was there was almost without a parallel. In the coldest and darkest nights of winter the rude chapels were crowded, and at the call for penitents hundreds would come down in sorrow and tears. . .Dalton was the spiritual birthplace of thousands." Prim pg 168

It's reported that General John B. Gordon attended the baptismal service of many converts within his ranks while being exposed to enemy fire. The Rapidan River

136

among many others, including many ponds served as convenient sites for the ordinance of baptism for thousands of 'soldiers in gray' that were following their Lord in outward testimony by their obedience to His Word.

"When orders came to march northward—on to Gettysburg—Hyman was in the water baptizing fifty-eight converts." Prim pg 102

Among the many Christian workers, pastors, evangelists, and colporteurs that were actively engaged in the preaching and dissemination of the Gospel in the Confederate Army, there would be no way to arrive at a definite count as to the number of converts. Only heaven itself contains the accurate record of each conversion and the impact that they made in the camps and the lasting effect that they made upon succeeding generations. There was several missionary type organizations formed under the auspices of either independent mission boards or well established denominational churches.

The churches that were the most active in providing Gospel literature, Bibles and chaplains to travel with the army were the Baptists, Presbyterian, Methodists and Episcopal. The official publications of these churches were very actively engaged in soliciting funds for support to help sponsor the chaplains and to buy more Gospel tracts and Bibles for the soldiers.

Many of the soldiers themselves sent offerings out of their $11.00 a month salary to mission Boards and Bible Societies to buy literature for the soldiers in other camps.

The Word of God was in the camp.

One of the most prominent Confederate chaplains that played a major part in spreading the Gospel throughout the Southern armies was William W. Bennett, D.D. He also held the position of Superintendent of "The Soldiers' Tract

> *"Knowing that intercessory prayer is our mightiest weapon and the supreme call for all Christians today, I pleadingly urge our people everywhere to pray. Believing that prayer is the greatest contribution that our people can make in this critical hour, I humbly urge that we take time to pray-- to really pray. "Knowing that intercessory prayer is our mightiest weapon and the supreme call for all*
>
> *Let there be prayer at sunup, at noonday, at sundown, at midnight -- all through the day. Let us pray for our children, our youth, our aged, our pastors, our homes. Let us pray for our churches.*
>
> *Let us pray for ourselves that we may not lose the word "concern" out of our Christian vocabulary. Let us pray for our nation. Let us pray for those who have never known Jesus Christ and redeeming love, for moral forces everywhere, for our national leaders. Let prayer be our passion. Let prayer be our practice."*
>
> *General Robert E. Lee*

Association." In his book entitled "Narrative of the Great Revival which Prevailed in the Southern Armies," he states, *". . . up to January, 1865 it was estimated that nearly one hundred and fifty thousand soldiers had been converted during the progress of the war, and it was believed that fully one-third of all the soldiers in the field were praying men and members of some branch of the Christian Church. A large proportion of the higher officers were men of faith and prayer, and many others, though not professedly religious, were moral, respectful to all the religious services and confessed the value of the revival in promoting the efficiency of the army."*

Dr. J. William Jones, in his record states that according to his estimate there were at least 50,000 converts in General Lee's army alone. It was reported by hospital staff workers, ministers, officers and visitors that among many of the patients in hospitals and convalescent houses, that strong conviction of sin would sweep over the soldiers. On many occasions they would seek a minister to talk to or pray with; sometimes, soldiers would spontaneously begin to praise and worship God or sing an old familiar hymn that would spread to many others in the house. **There was singing in the camp.**

In spite of the most deplorable conditions that existed in the Northern prisons, such as Point Lookout, Fort Delaware, Elmira and Johnson's Island, hundreds of southern soldiers found Christ as their Savior while confined to such prison surroundings.

> ". . . I would cry, 'men of Israel! Help!'"
>
> ---Rev. H.G. Crews

Thousands of the soldier converts that survived the war later enrolled in seminary schools in the southern states. As many of these Christian soldiers returned home, either during or after the war, their living testimonies for

Christ would inflame their churches and home towns with greater zeal for the Gospel of Christ. Hundreds of these young men graduated from Bible colleges and seminaries as pastors, evangelists, and missionaries that would later impact not only the South, but also Northern states and in some cases the world for Jesus Christ. Hundreds of churches were established and pastored by these 'southern soldier boys' and some of them, in turn, would be future leaders in evangelical Christianity.

During the process of the war, the call was made by officers and overworked chaplains for help in the camps. Rev. H. G. Crews wrote from Winchester, VA in his appeal for help by saying, *"Oh, it is a blessed work to care for the souls of our brave boys. If I could reach the ear of every Christian in the Confederacy, I would cry "men of Israel! help!"".* Dr. Rosser, a Chaplain who was laboring among the camps of General Ewell's corps wrote, *"we want our best men here - holy men - hardworking men - sympathizing men - self-denying men - men baptized afresh every day by the Holy Ghost for the work."*

The chaplains that answered the call of God for such a work were men of dedication and zeal to preach the Word, men of passion who desired to see genuine conversions and men of deep conviction that realized in the inner recesses of their soul that Divine destiny had designed such an hour in the history of their nation. As one soldier writes from the battlefield in describing the church in the army says *that ". . . the great theme will be the twin duties - Piety and Patriotism. . . our cause has been already baptized in the blood of Christian patriots."* Thank God for holy men of real dedication and deep conviction that served our soldiers in the camp!

"The chaplain-historian J. Williams Jones wrote of the chaplain and his sermons:

'Whoever it is, he preaches the Gospel. He does not discuss the 'relations of science to religion,' or the slavery question, or the causes which led to the war itself. He does not indulge in abusive epithets of the invaders of our soil, or seek to fire his hearers with hatred or vindictiveness toward the enemy. He is looking in the eyes of Heroes of many a battle, and knows that the 'long roll may beat in the midst of his sermon and summon the men to battle and to death, and therefore he speaks as a dying man to dying men,' talking with great earnestness 'the old, old story of salvation." Prim pg 10

Many of the army chaplains would not only preach in fine structured church buildings, but also in quickly constructed chapels built by the soldiers or even held meetings in the trenches. One writer from General Lee's Army wrote that *"frequent prayer meetings have been held in the trenches, and even on the advance skirmish line, within easy musket range of the enemy, the song of praise and the voice of supplication have been heard. Sermons have also been preached in the trenches - albeit, they have sometimes been cut short by the bursting of the shell or the whistling of the minnie."*

The army chaplains and visiting pastors and evangelists who ministered in the camps were highly qualified both spiritually and physically to meet the demanding challenges that they had to face while presenting the Gospel message to the soldiers under such difficult conditions. These dedicated men of God would stay with the army for months on end in all types of weather and endure the struggles with the common soldiers from one campaign to another. One officer of the Eighteenth Virginia Cavalry, assigned to Imboden's Brigade wrote that *just "before the charge, and while we were in line, the command to dismount was given when our noble chaplain sang a hymn and then prayed, the whole regiment kneeling. It was a solemn and impressive sight just on the eve of battle, and God blessed our arms with victory."* **There was humility in the camp.**

"One colporteur observed that tracts tended to increase moral and religious feelings among the soldiers.

"Stonewall Jackson Preparing For Battle"

General Ewell -- "If that is religion, I must have it."

One chaplain stated that he had never seen anything at home like the soldiers' demands for religious printed materials. He thought that all other chaplains and distributors would concur with his opinion. The great demand indicated that there was an opening for evangelism by the press.

"The word of God in the form of a pocket Bible or Testament, was the first thing sought after, and the hymn-book came next; but it was generally necessary . . . only to show one's self, with a pocket of tracts or religious papers, in the corner of an encampment and begin to give them out, and you would be very soon surrounded by an eager crowd, asking for something to read." Prim pg 29

"J.W. Jones said of his own experience:

> I had a pair of large saddle bags which I used to pack with tracts and religious newspapers, and with Bibles and Testaments . . . Thus equipped I would sally forth and as I drew near the camp someone would raise the cry, 'Yonder comes the Bible and tract man,' and such crowds would rush out to meet me that frequently I would sit on my horse and distribute my supply before I even got into the camp . . .The poor fellows would crowd around and beg for them as earnestly as if they were golden guineas." Prim. Pg 31

Prayer meetings were held everywhere in the camps. Some meetings were conducted by officers, some by common soldiers as well as by ministers. They were held in the trenches, around camp fires, in crudely constructed chapels, under trees, on the river banks, as well as in open fields. The Spirit of God was truly being poured out upon *"your sons"* as prophesied by the prophet Joel (Joel 2:28). **Truly, there was joy in the camp.**

> "One colporteur wrote: "Many a time, officers and privates who made no profession of religion gathered around him at night, listening with undisguised pleasure to the reading of God's words, and joined in the sweet old songs of Zion until the forest rang again with their grateful praise." Prim pg 27

> "The sanctuary was always crowded and loud, animated singing always hailed his approach. All the soldiers 'leaned upon the voice of the preacher' as if

God Himself had called them together to hear of life and death eternal." Prim pg 91

During the winter months of 1864-65 when General Lee and his 30,000 remaining troops were holding their line against General Grant's overwhelming numbers, religious activities were a big part of the Army of Northern Virginia. Along the Confederate's 40 miles of entrenchments, the soldiers and officers had built about 60 chapels. It was reported that sometimes one could stand in one spot and hear two or three religious meetings going on at the same time.

> "Private John Dooley wrote that during the calm periods, the preachers were indefatigable in their efforts to draw the soldiers together to sing psalms and to pray. Hundreds and thousands responded to their call and the woods resounded for miles around with the earnest music of Lee's veterans." Prim pg 94

The singing of old familiar hymns was a clarion call for worship and also an invitation for the Holy Spirit to take complete control of the meeting and draw men to the living Savior. On many occasions the words of an old hymn such as "How Firm a Foundation" or "Am I a Soldier of the Cross" would fill the air coming from the hearts and voices blended together in heavenly harmony in spontaneous response to the overwhelming presence of God in the midst of a rag-tag crowd of southern soldiers. In winter's cold or summer's heat, in sunshine or in rain -- it mattered not -- could be heard the words being sweetly sung, "When I Can Read My Title Clear" or "All Hail the Power of Jesus Name" rising unto God in praise as one voice coming from the hearts of fighting men who knew their Savior. *Truly, there was joy in the camp, because Jesus Himself was in their midst.*

There was a remarkable response from the southern Christians back home as reports of revival began to be heard in the local churches. Rev. J.C. Granberry reported that he collected five thousand and seven thousand dollars from two separate Petersburg, Virginia Methodist churches for the support of the revival. Many a saint back home eager to help support such a worthy cause while burning with a heartfelt passion for lost souls would willingly part with their own personal Bible, coupled with a generous offering and send it to the soldiers on the front line.

On April 8, 1864, General Robert E. Lee issued orders for his troops to observe the "day of fasting, humiliation, and prayer" that had been proclaimed by President Jefferson Davis:

"Soldiers! Let us humble ourselves before the Lord, our God, asking through Christ, the forgiveness of our sins, beseeching the aid of the God of our forefathers in the defense of our homes and our liberties, thanking Him for His past blessings, and imploring their continuance upon our cause and our people."

During these trying times several Bible Societies were formed to help finance, secure and provide Bibles and Gospel tracts for distribution. When Bibles and Gospel literature were in short supply or could no longer be obtained from northern publishers these Bible Societies with the overwhelming approval of the Congress of the Confederate States of America would have thousands of Bibles and tracts imported from England. Often British Bible Societies would make large donations free of charge.

One of the most remarkable characteristics of this revival is the number of genuine Christian men that were among the highest ranking officers in the army. Many of the officers who distinguished themselves in heroic deeds of valor throughout the war were Christians from the outset. Some of the most well-known among them were Robert E. Lee, T. J. (Stonewall) Jackson, Kirby Smith, J.E.B. Stuart, W.N. Pendleton and many others too numerous to mention.

General Robert E. Lee was a man who had a deep abiding faith in the Lord Jesus Christ as his personal Savior. He would often make mention of his utmost confidence in the sovereignty of God in both the triumphs and tragedies of his life. After the war he accepted the presidency of the Rockbridge Bible Society of Lexington, Virginia and freely gave much support in time and money to the purchase and distribution of Bibles and Christian literature.

It was common knowledge among the officers and privates alike of General Stonewall Jackson's Christian faith and sanctified lifestyle as a child of God. General Jackson never entered a fight without first asking for divine guidance, blessing and protection. He was a strong believer in keeping the Sabbath day holy, so therefore, many times he was very reluctant to fight or travel on that day. Generals Polk was a bishop, Pendleton, an Episcopal clergyman, and D.H. Hill a Christian writer.

The accounts are too numerous indeed to mention about the officers that were outstanding examples of Christian character and the life-changing grace of God. Also there were a good number of high-ranking officers who professed Christ for the first time while serving in the Confederate Army. In many cases they were influenced and led to Christ by their fellow officers. There were many reports of Christian officers such as Stonewall Jackson who would attend and take an active part in the religious meetings with his men. On many occasions he himself would conduct the service when a chaplain was not available.

" I am alone in the world"

In recounting the history of this great revival in the Confederate Army and even among the civilian population, is not to imply that everyone was or became a Christian or that all evil was eradicated from our land. As we look back in retrospect upon this epoch event, it is very obvious that our sovereign God used this spiritual awakening to help preserve the South in spite of its military defeat. The Lord sent this mighty revival at this particular time to prepare the South for the disaster that it would suffer during the war and the toil and turbulence that it would have to endure in the ten long years of reconstruction. The Lord, no doubt, sent this mighty revival not only to sustain the people of the South in their temporary suffering and struggle to recover from the ravages of war, but also to preserve the strong godly convictions of the Protestant Christian Faith that were so deeply rooted in the hearts of the people. The Holy Ghost was poured out in fulfillment of the prophecy of Joel in not only a saving power for the people living during that era, but for the spiritual welfare of generations yet nborn.

"Bennett closed his narrative of the revivals with the question—

"Were the fruits of the army revivals enduring?" To this question, he replied that thousands, in 1877, could give an affirmative response. "In all the churches of the South there are earnest, devout, and active Christians, who date their spiritual birth from some revival in Virginia, in the West, or in the far South."

"In glowing terms he spoke of the effect of revivals: Strange as it may seem to many readers, the call to preach the gospel of Christ came to the hearts of the men of war on the tented field; and no sooner were their carnal weapons laid aside than they buckled on the Divine armor, and seizing the sword of the Spirit, entered the battle against the powers of darkness. In this we find one of the strongest proofs of the genuineness of the Army Revival. Truly, its fruits are still enduring. Thousands who were participants in that glorious and, to some, strange work, have passed the gloom of death and are seen no more among men, but the seed they sowed in trench and camp and hospital, in the bivouac, and on the weary march, was watered from above and has borne a rich harvest. And may we not hope that the full fruition of this work is to be realized in that era of peace and good will which is even now descending upon our common country?" Prim pg 216

There have been many outpourings of God's Holy Spirit since that revival among the 'soldiers in gray' that have resulted in the salvation of multiplied thousands throughout both the North and the South. Many churches have been established, young men called into Christian ministry and missionary endeavors even to this present day as the Word of God has been preached by the sons and grandsons of those men whose lives were transformed by the power of the Gospel while fighting for their country. Surely, the God of Jacob was keeping His promise to His children as given by the prophet Isaiah, *". . . and the Redeemer shall come to Zion, and unto them that turn from transgression in Jacob, saith the Lord. As for me this is my covenant with them, saith the Lord, my Spirit that is upon thee, and my words which I have put in thy mouth, shall not depart out of thy mouth, nor out of the mouth of thy seed, nor out of the mouth of thy seed's seed, saith the Lord, from henceforth and forever."* (Isaiah 59:20-21)

"The Rev. J. Williams Jones, a Baptist evangelist who labored to promote revivalism in the camps of General Lee's Army of Northern Virginia, spoke of the 'God of Israel, God of the centuries, God of our forefathers, God of Jefferson Davis and Sidney Johnston and Robert E. Lee and Stonewall Jackson, and God of the Southern Confederacy.' The Confederacy was the latest successor to the ancient

Hebrews in having a unique place in the providence of God." Southern Sermons pg 223

When the tired fighting men of General Lee's Army of Northern Virginia laid down their arms and furled their glorious flag for the last time at Appomattox, VA, admitting military defeat, little did they realize that within them God had won a great spiritual victory for His people and for the survival of this great nation. What a loss they suffered on the battlefield, but what a victory they had won at their altars. In the mind of our omniscient God, He knew that a standard of righteousness had to be raised in the face of the flood of political and economic corruption, moral debauchery, intellectual and philosophical atheism, and spiritual infidelity that would arise again during the last half of the nineteenth century and would persist even to this present day. Isaiah again prophesied that ". . . *when the enemy shall come in like a flood, the Spirit of the Lord shall lift up a standard against him"* (Isaiah 59:19).

"The Bible is a book, in comparison with which all others in my eyes are of minor importance."

--General Robert E. Lee

We today can truly offer praise unto our God for His faithfulness in keeping His covenant promises to His people Israel and to their literal descendants. Multiplied millions of Americans today both of the North and the South can trace their ancestry back to the ancient Celts located in the British Isles that tenaciously contended for the faith "once delivered to the saints." Our Anglo-Saxon Celtic ancestors were in turn descended from the ancient Israelites of the Diaspora (dispersion) from Palestine in the 7th century B.C. It is no mystery why the Lord in His unlimited mercy poured out His Spirit even among such a humble rag-tag group of men as those in the Southern Army. He was keeping His covenant promises to our ancient forefathers of Old Testament history.

With the passing of 135 years of time and events, of prosperity and depression, of peace and world wars, of triumphs and tragedies in our nation; we can no longer hear the preaching of those chaplains in the trenches, the rejoicing during the baptismal ordinances in our rivers and creeks, the cries of repentance and the worship loudly offered unto God from the lips of hardened soldiers newly born again of the Spirit of God; but this one thing we can surely say, "their echoes still remain."

Illustrations from the book:
CHRIST IN THE CAMP
by J. William Jones, D.D.
Chaplain, Confederate Army
Available from Sprinkle Publications
Harrisonburg, Virginia

CHAPLAINS OF THE CONFEDERACY

There was an untold number of "men of God" who served in various capacities among the ranks of the Confederate soldiers. Among them were pastors of local churches, evangelists, colporteurs and chaplains. There were about 600 known chaplains that served their respective military units. Some even served in the dual capacity of an officer or surgeon. These men were welcomed into the ranks both by the commanding officers and the common soldiers. They served as vital instruments of Christ in the great spiritual revival which transpired in the Confederate Army.

I am both proud and humbled to mention the name of Chaplain Thomas C. Jennings who faithfully served the Eleventh Virginia Regiment in respectfully acknowledging our family name and ancestral state of Virginia.

The following accounts are only three among many of the outstanding "men of God" who served their Savior, country and people during a time of unspeakable national hardships and tragedies.

REV. MOSES DRURY HOGE, D.D.

FAITHFUL PASTOR, EDITOR, COMPASSIONATE CHAPLAIN, DEVOTED SUPPORTER OF HIS COUNTRY AND DEFENDER OF THE CHRISTIAN FAITH

In order to get an accurate picture of the life and times of the Southern people just prior to and during the War for Southern Independence, one must consider the nature of southern religion and its clergy. The institution of Southern Protestantism and the strong influence of the Christian clergy were two of the major factors that molded southern social and political values for sixty years prior to the war. While Northern Unitarianism waged its war of idealism against the South, the South waged its defensive war against Northern liberal religion in order to preserve its conservative Protestant heritage.

Of all the historical accounts of the War for Southern Independence, only a small amount deals with its religious and spiritual aspects. Yet, in some respects this war was as much a religious crusade, as it was a military campaign. "A more religious war was never waged by any nation than that now entered upon by the southern people," wrote the editor of the Richmond Dispatch in June 1861. During this trying time of national turmoil, there were many southern Christian ministers that displayed unusual courage and were a source of moral encouragement and spiritual guidance throughout the war. Moses Drury Hoge was one such noble man of God who faithfully served his fellow citizens and the cause of the Confederacy.

Moses Drury Hoge was born on September 18, 1818 in Prince Edward County, Virginia to Hampden-Sydney College Vice President Samuel Davies Hoge and his wife Elizabeth. Samuel Hoge moved his family to Athens, Ohio in 1820, but was there only six years before passing away. Moses went to live with his uncle, Drury Lacy in New Bern, NC in 1836 and entered Hampden-Sydney College in the fall. He graduated as Valedictorian of his class in 1839. After several months he then entered Union Theological Seminary in Prince Edward County as a ministerial student. In 1843 he accepted the call as assistant to the pastor of the First Presbyterian Church of Richmond, VA. In 1845, with the help of his denomination, Dr. Hoge became founder and pastor of Richmond's Second Presbyterian Church where he faithfully remained for fifty-four years.

Rev. Hoge soon became very active in serving not only the members of the church, but also the citizens of the city. In 1848 he established a school for girls and served as Headmaster until 1852. His denominational duties included preaching, traveling, lecturing and conducting revival services. In the late 1840's Rev. Hoge, with his friend Rep. James McDowell, was instrumental in pushing through a bill in the U.S. House of Representatives that would allow chaplains in every regiment of the army. He stated "I have thus been the humble instrument in originating an action which has resulted in the appointment of chaplains for every regiment whereas before there were none". He was a man that was held in high esteem not only for his intellectual abilities, his untiring service to the people, his sincere conviction and dedication to God's Word, but his leadership qualities and was therefore offered the presidency of two southern colleges. He declined both offers in order to remain as pastor in Richmond.

Among his various endeavors, Dr. Hoge was deeply interested in politics. As an outlet for expressing his political views, he became editor of the Central Presbyterian, a religious journal with a moderate political format. As editor, Dr. Hoge often expressed his unionist feelings and his opposition to secession. He condemned the abuses of slavery and the idea of reopening the African slave trade while denouncing the extremes of northern abolitionism. Due to the North's extreme radical Republicanism and liberal interpretation of the Constitution, Dr. Hoge became a strong supporter of his home state when it seceded in early 1861.

Early on, Dr. Hoge was intensely interested in ministerial work among the soldiers in the Confederate Army. Governor John Letcher soon appointed him to the Council for Chaplains. He became a regular preacher at the Camp of Instruction in Richmond and preached to over 100,000 men during the course of the war. He soon became a favorite speaker among the soldiers of the Stonewall Brigade. Corporal James P. Smith records:

"One Sunday afternoon, by our invitation, Dr. Hoge drove out to preach in the camp of the Stonewall Brigade. How well I remember the great assembly of young soldiers, seated on the ground like the five thousand at Bethsaida, in companies . . . the sermon I have no distinct recollection, but the prayer, with far reaching distinctness and with appeal and tenderness went up through the open skies to the God of so many fathers and mothers, to the great Captain of our Salvation, and went down into the hearts of those boys in gray and tears were on many faces and strong desires in many hearts. Near the preacher, on a log, sat Stonewall Jackson, and with him a circle of men of rank and on one side a choir of boys who knew their hymns well."

Dr. Hoge was so dedicated to the cause and the soldiers of the Confederacy that he returned to the Secretary of War $300.00 which was the amount of his pay as chaplain for six months. In addition to his other duties, Dr. Hoge served as "honorary chaplain" of the Confederate Congress at the request of Vice President Alexander H. Stephens. He opened the sessions of the Congress with prayer forty-four times, far exceeding any other minister.

On December 13, 1862 Dr. Hoge's brother, William, a Presbyterian minister in Charlottesville, suggested writing a letter to the Christians of Great Britain. In it he would appeal for Bibles, Testaments, tracts and other religious publications to be distributed to the officers and soldiers of the Southern Army. Dr. Hoge was appointed by the Virginia Bible Society to visit the British and Foreign Bible Society and request a procurement of 35,000 Bibles and Testaments. This plan met with swift approval from many churchmen, Confederate Cabinet members and the Southern Presbyterian Committee of Publication.

> "I invited him (Dr. Hoge) to Camp Winder to preach for us. Without hesitation he consented to do so. Rain, hail or shine, every Sunday night he was at his post, preaching and visiting the sick, giving words of comfort and encouragement. I say this, If the Confederate soldier ever had a friend, that friend is Dr. Hoge. To this day the old veterans love him."
>
> --A Confederate Veteran 1895

Dr. Hoge left Richmond by train on December 23, 1862 bound for Charleston, SC. From there, the steamer upon which he was aboard, after running the Union naval blockade, took him to the West Indies. From there they set sail for England on January 14, 1863.

On February 16 Dr. Hoge met with the board of managers of the British and Foreign Bible Society and presented to them the need of the Southern Army for Bibles and Gospel literature. The Society graciously granted his request by making a free grant of 10,000 Bibles, 50,000 Testaments and 250,000 Gospels and Psalms estimated in value of $20,000. The London Tract Society also gave him $1500 worth of their publications. The first load of Bibles was sent from England that same month and arrived in Charleston in June and from there were transported to Richmond. Due to the Union naval blockade it is estimated that 75 percent of the books reached the Confederate

Capital. Inspired by Dr. Hoge's mission, the American Bible Society donated more than 50,000 Bibles to the South.

Uncertain as to the safety of his return trip he wrote; "a few days will determine whether my destination will be the bottom of the sea, Richmond or some Northern Bastille". Under enemy fire, aboard the blockade-runner the "Advance" he safely arrived at Wilmington, NC on October 11, 1863. Dr. Hoge remained faithful to the cause of the Confederacy until the very end. He returned to his work as army chaplain for the remainder of the war. He continued as pastor for the next 30 years serving his parishioners and veterans by visiting and preaching at Soldier's Homes.

At 80 years of age Dr. Hoge was injured in a streetcar accident and never recovered from his injuries. He died on January 6, 1899 and was buried in Richmond's Hollywood Cemetery. His biographer, Payton Hoge wrote this tribute:

"And there he sleeps...with the great and heroic dead of Virginia and the Confederacy, to who he so often had paid eloquent tribute; in the soil of the Virginia he so loyally served and so devotedly loved."

Second Presbyterian Church, Richmond, Virginia

CHARLES TODD QUINTARD, M.D.

MAN OF LEARNING, COMPASSIONATE PHYSICIAN AND SURGEON, BELOVED CHAPLAIN, EPISCOPAL BISHOP, EDUCATOR AND HUMBLE CHRISTIAN SERVANT.

During the War for Southern Independence, the religious nature of Southern culture was one of the motivating forces which empowered the Southern people in their struggle against Northern aggression. Many of the South's most prominent Christian ministers often equated religious fervor with patriotic fervor. The dual qualities of 'piety and patriotism' were not options, but an absolute necessary part of the average Confederate soldier's 'equipment' on the battlefield. The most distinguishing difference between the Northern and Southern soldiers was not only *__how__* they fought, but *__why__* they fought. The Northern soldier was fighting for what he thought was the preservation of the Union. The Union was that vague impersonal and invisible entity which they conceived as their form of government with all its functions headquartered in Washington, D.C.

The Southern soldier answered a call not only from his country, but his conscience. He fought to preserve a way of life which was enjoyed by his ancestors and hopefully he could pass on to his descendants. Among the thousands of Southern men who answered the call to arms, scores of Christian ministers also felt their patriotic duty to serve the cause of the South. One such minister to serve, not only his country, but the physical and spiritual needs of his fellow countrymen was Charles Todd Quintard.

Dr. Quintard was born into a prominent Stamford, Connecticut family of French Huguenot ancestry on December 22, 1824. His father, Isaac Quintard was a man of wealth and education. As a young man, Dr. Quintard attended Trinity School, New York City and then earned his master's degree at Columbia College. He then earned a degree in medicine, at the University of the City of New York in 1847. After serving a year in Bellevue Hospital, he moved to Athens, Georgia and began his practice of medicine. He moved to Memphis, Tennessee in 1851 and became professor of Physiology and Pathological Anatomy in the Medical College.

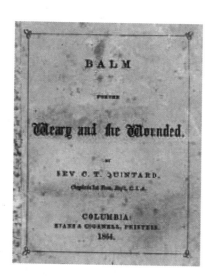

Dr. Quintard wrote this booklet for the comfort of the wounded soldiers of the First Tennessee Regiment.

In January 1854 Dr. Quintard became a candidate for Holy Orders in the Episcopal Church of the Diocese of Tennessee. He soon became an avid student of theology under the direction of Bishop Otey and was first a deacon in 1855 and then a member of the priesthood soon afterward. For the next several years he served as rector in Memphis and Nashville parishes and soon became a prominent and popular preacher known throughout the Diocese of Tennessee. Dr. Quintard possessed a magnetic personality and a pleasant disposition which attracted both young and old and thereby enabled him to minister to the physical and spiritual needs of many people.

Due to his righteous influence over the young men of the city of Nashville, *the **Rock City Guard,*** a militia company, elected Dr. Quintard as their Chaplain. Being a spiritual leader with deep affection and concern for the welfare of the enlisting military men of his parish, he

163

willingly accepted the chaplaincy of the First Tennessee Regiment. In 1861, he left the care and comforts of his Nashville home and parish to serve the needs of his fellow countrymen on the battlefield. He never returned to his home in Nashville until after the end of the war in 1865. While faithfully serving as Chaplain of his regiment, he saw action in Kentucky, Cheat Mountain, Munfordville, Perryville, Murfreesboro, Chickamauga and Franklin.

Dr. Quintard was a chaplain that displayed genuine Christian concern and compassion for all the men under his charge. As a medical doctor, he exercised utmost care in executing the duties of his profession. After the battle of Perryville he recalls, "When the wounded were brought to the rear, at 3 o'clock in the afternoon, I took my place as a surgeon on Chaplain's Creek and throughout the rest of the day and until half past five the next morning, without food of any sort, I was incessantly occupied with the wounded. It was a horrible night I spent, God save me from such another. I suppose excitement kept me up. About half past five in the morning of the 9th, I dropped, - I could do no more. I went out by myself and leaning against a fence, I wept like a child. And all that day I was so unnerved that if any one asked me about the regiment, I could make no reply without tears. Having taken off my shirt to tear into strips to make bandages, I took a severe cold."

With unequaled dedication to the Confederate cause and to the men to whom he was called to serve, he endured many severe hardships without complaint. On many occasions he would march ten to fifteen miles or even give up his horse to a less fortunate officer or private who was suffering from sore blistered feet, injury or fatigue. Sleeping on the ground with only a blanket for protection was a common practice. Often times, he would sleep in torrential rains and would be soaked to the skin. In freezing temperatures, his blanket and clothes would be covered with ice. Many nights were spent without a camp fire in fear of enemy detection. It was common for proper food to be in short supply as he recalls in his ***Personal Narrative***.

> *"I had no provisions, but various persons gave me what made up a tolerably good supper, to wit, - a roasting ear, a slice of bacon and a biscuit; and in the morning I found on a log a good-sized piece of fresh meat, not strikingly clean, but I sliced off a piece of it and cooked it on a long stick. The fire, I reckon, removed all impurities; and Joe Van Leer brought me half a cup of coffee and another biscuit."*

Dr. Quintard was a personal friend to many high-ranking Confederate officers and was instrumental in leading some of them to faith in Christ, including General Braxton Bragg. He was widely accepted, deeply loved and appreciated by both the military and civilian population everywhere he went. He ministered to both privates and Generals, friend and foe, whenever and wherever he could spread the message of the love of God and the transforming power of Jesus Christ, the Redeemer. In recalling his ministry in the Confederate Army he said,

> *"I was very glad to believe that my labors among the soldiers as their chaplain were not all thrown away. It was very delightful to see how well our regular daily evening service in camp was attended...One of the Captains told the major that he believed every man in his company would lay down his life for me. Certainly I met nothing but kindness from the officers and men. And so I was*

led to hope that some good would grow out of the seed sown in those wild mountains."

After the war, Dr. Quintard was elected Bishop of Tennessee in 1865 and served in that Diocese for thirty-three years. He soon set about in the establishment of schools and especially the University of the South in Sewanee, TN. He traveled to England to raise funds for the school and while there received several honors. The LL.D. degree was conferred on him at the University of Cambridge; he preached at the Royal Chapel at Windsor and was made Chaplain of the Order of St. John of Jerusalem.

After a life of service and dedication to his parishioners, his country and his Savior, Dr. Quintard entered his eternal rest at Darien, GA on February 15, 1898, and was buried in the Sewanee, Tennessee cemetery.

Sources: Dr. Quintard - Chaplain C.S.A and Second Bishop of Tennessee and Chaplains in Gray.

REV. EDWARD M. BOUNDS

LAWYER, FAITHFUL PASTOR, ARMY CHAPLAIN, DEVOTIONAL WRITER, BELOVED HUSBAND-FATHER, POWERFUL PREACHER AND A MAN OF FERVENT PRAYER

For forty years immediately preceding the War for Southern Independence, the young American republic was experiencing a social and spiritual turmoil that resulted in a blood-bath that would be unequaled in its history. The nature of that national tragedy would be a deep struggle for the very life and soul of its people and would determine the direction of its political, social and spiritual destiny. Those were times that brought out the worst traits and evil deeds of some men while it demanded the courageous display of sterling character and noble deeds of others.

> "Man is looking for better methods. God is looking for better men, Men are God's methods.
>
> E.M. Bounds

The whole social and cultural structure of the South was under attack from Northern literary liberals and political radicals. These self-appointed social reformers launched their repeated attacks intending to break the tenacious will of the Southern people while destroying the last stronghold of Biblical Christianity in America. It was during those dark days of political unrest and cultural turmoil that God raised up a man of deep spiritual insight, unrelenting faith and unequaled passion for the purity of the Gospel of Jesus Christ. E.M. Bounds was that dedicated and humble servant of God who lived his whole life to please his Savior and to serve his fellow man.

Edward McKendree Bounds was born on August 15, 1835 to Thomas J. and Hatty Bounds in Shelby County, Missouri. His father was a successful businessman and a Christian layman who was instrumental in building the ***First Methodist Church*** in Shelbyville in 1840. At the age of forty-four in the year 1849 T.J. Bounds contracted tuberculosis and died when Edward was only fourteen years old. At the funeral service young Edward began his search to know God in a more personal way.

Soon after his father's death, Edward and his elder brother Charles traveled to Mesquite Canyon in California in hopes of making a fortune in gold mining. Their excitement soon turned to hard work and disappointment as they observed the moral degradation and rugged living conditions of their fellow miners. After four unsuccessful years they left and returned to Missouri. Young Edward studied law in Hannibal, Missouri and at the age of twenty-one became the state's youngest practicing lawyer.

The revival fire of the **Great Spiritual Awakening** of 1857-58 had now reached northern Missouri and was soon to change Edward's life. The Methodist Episcopal Church South in La Grange sponsored a brush arbor meeting with Evangelist Smith Thomas. It was during these meetings that the Spirit of God moved mightily upon Edward's heart and he answered God's call for full-time Christian ministry. Soon afterward, he enrolled in Centenary Seminary of the M.E. Church South in Palmyra, MO. Two years later he graduated and received his ministerial preaching circuit.

On May 10, 1861 Union troops captured the Missouri Arsenal at St. Louis and made prisoners of the State Guard. That afternoon Union Troops murdered twenty-eight civilians in the **St. Louis Massacre**. While pastoring in Brunswick, MO, Rev. Bounds officiated the funeral of a seventeen year old boy who was falsely accused and drowned by Union soldiers in the frozen Grand River. He witnessed the merciless execution of 55 non-combatants by Union troops and preached the funeral of one of the victims of the **Palmyra Massacre**. Witnessing these brutal atrocities and understanding the unconstitutional position of the Federal government, Rev. Bounds refused to sign the **Oath of Allegiance**. Considered as a spy, he was arrested along with 249 others and was imprisoned in the Jefferson Barracks at St. Louis. After enduring despicable prison conditions for a month and a half, he was ordered to leave the state and not to return. As a prisoner he was taken to Memphis on a Federal boat and then to Washington, AR to a prisoner exchange camp. After his release, he walked over 200 miles to Pine Bluff where be bought a mule and continued traveling east in search of his friend, General Sterling Price. On February 7, 1863 he joined the Confederate Army and was assigned to Company B of the Third Missouri Infantry. Rev. Bounds faithfully served his fellow soldiers as chaplain. He did not hide from danger but remained at the front lines of battle. He witnessed first-hand all the horrors, fear, pain, agony and death of war. Between campaigns, Chaplain Bounds would conduct religious services in local churches where many civilians and soldiers accepted the bountiful grace of the Savior and were born into the Kingdom of God.

Against the advice of other chaplains, Rev. Bounds remained in Vicksburg during the siege and ministered to the suffering citizens and soldiers. As chaplain, he continued to share the grace of God with officers and privates while in the campaigns of Mississippi, Alabama and Georgia. He was present at the outpouring of the Holy Spirit among soldiers and citizens alike. After the death of his friend, Bishop/General Leonidas Polk, he and Chaplain Charles Quintard accompanied the body on the train to Marietta, GA to deliver it to Mrs. Polk and her daughter. Rev. Bounds later endured the battle of Atlanta and the devastating massacre at Franklin, TN where he suffered a severe forehead injury from a Union saber. After the battle of Franklin, Rev. Bounds was taken to Nashville and held in the Tennessee State Penitentiary until he pledged his allegiance to the Union on June 28, 1865.

Rev. Bounds then returned to the city of Franklin and became pastor of the Methodist Church. There he had previously preached with love and tears the message of the Savior during the war. Revival fire fell among the city for weeks and 150 people made public confession of faith in Christ. He also served pastorates in Selma and Eufaula, Alabama and St. Louis, Missouri, while continuing to hold evangelistic meetings. His writing and passionate preaching resulted in a close friendship with the famous evangelist, Sam Jones.

On September 19, 1876, at the age of forty-one, he was married to Emma Elizabeth Barnett. God richly blessed this marriage with three lovely children. Nine years later at the age of thirty, his beloved wife, Emmie, died on February 18, 1886. After twenty months of grief and heartache, he married Harriet A. Barnett, a cousin to his first wife. He was now fifty-two years old. The Lord again blessed them with four children, but tragedy struck when Rev. Bound's son Edward became sick and died. Then his son Charles, by his second wife, died at one year and eight days old.

On June 7, 1890 Rev. Bounds assumed his new duty as Assistant Editor of the M.E. Church South official publication, the *Christian Advocate*. By this time many members wanted the National Conference to take a strong stand against worldliness. Due to his beliefs on strict holiness standards and his position favoring the role of evangelists in the church, Bounds resigned his position four years later. He quietly left the *Christian Advocate*, refusing any retirement pay and moved his family to Washington, GA. Rev. Bounds had been like a weeping prophet to his Methodist Church whose leadership was now bent on compromise and profit. His invitations for ministry had stopped and he was now rejected by the National Conference. He then began to receive invitations for ministry from outside his Methodist Church. Wherever he preached the throngs gathered, the heavenly fire descended and hundreds found themselves under conviction of sin and confessing their new-found faith in Jesus Christ.

Among the many honorable Christian traits of this Godly saint was his sincere humility. He never sought praise for any service rendered even when it was rightly deserved. When *Southern University* of Greensboro, AL desired to confer on him an Honorary Doctorate of Divinity degree, he kindly turned down this special honor with deep conviction and gratitude. For the last nineteen years of his life, E.M. Bounds gave himself to intercessory prayer. He was deeply burdened because of the backslidden condition of his Church, the lukewarmness of ministers, the moral decay of his nation and for the lost condition of his fellow-countrymen. He spent a minimum of three to four hours each morning in fervent prayer, prostrate before the throne of heaven. He truly communed with his God in close fellowship and deep conviction. As a result of his life of fervent prayer, he wrote eight books including his famous *"Preacher and Prayer"*. The earthly journey of this beloved saint of God came to an end on August 24, 1913, at his home in Washington GA at the age of seventy-eight.

"Revivals are among the charter rights of the Church . . .a revival means a heartbroken pastor. A revival means a church on its knees confessing its sins - the sins of the individual and of the Church - confessing the sins of the times and of the community."

E.M. Bounds

Deo Vindice
(God will vindicate)